DRIFTING TOWARDS ANOTHER CIVIL WAR IN AMERICA

DRIFTING TOWARDS ANOTHER CIVIL WAR IN AMERICA

DONALD KROPP

Algora Publishing
New York

Library of Congress Cataloging-in-Publication Data —

Names: Kropp, Donald, author.
Title: Drifting towards another civil war in America / Donald Kropp.
Description: New York: Algora Publishing, [2017] | Includes bibliographical
    references.
Identifiers: LCCN 2017016410 (print) | LCCN 2017020901 (ebook) | ISBN
    9781628942750 (pdf) | ISBN 9781628942736 (soft cover: alk. paper) | ISBN
    9781628942743 (hard cover: alk. paper)
Subjects: LCSH: Democracy—United States. | Political culture—United
States.
    | Ideology—United States. | Conservatism—United States. | Social
    values—United States. | United States—Politics and government. | United
    States—Social conditions.
Classification: LCC JK1726 (ebook) | LCC JK1726 .K76 2017 (print) | DDC
    306.20973—dc23
LC record available at https://lccn.loc.gov/2017016410

Printed in the United States

I dedicate this book to Steven Scott Shepherd,
whose family tradition was to serve in our military,
and to all of our veterans, of all of our wars.

TABLE OF CONTENTS

INTRODUCTION

1

CHAPTER 1: THE DECLINE OF REPRESENTATIVE GOVERNMENT
IN THE UNITED STATES 7

CHAPTER 2: THE SECRET ORDER CAME FROM GERMANY
IN 1832 19

CHAPTER 3: WHERE DID THE AMERICAN FASCIST FAMILIES
OF THE 1930S GO? 27

CHAPTER 4: WHY DID THE MEDIA FAIL TO PROTECT THE
PEOPLE? 37

CHAPTER 5: THE PEOPLE MUST BE LIED TO BEFORE THEY
CAN BE MOBILIZED 41

CHAPTER 6: A SOCIETY BUILT ON LIES EVENTUALLY DIES 49

CHAPTER 7: MESOPOTAMIA, DARFUR, AND SOMALIA, DESERVE
SOME EXAMINATION... 53

CHAPTER 8: ADVICE FOR OUR ENEMIES 57

CHAPTER 9: WHO TAUGHT AMERICANS HOW TO TORTURE?
WHEN?   63

CHAPTER 10: A SOCIAL COMMENTARY ON AMERICAN SOCIETY   67

CHAPTER 11: RETAIL AND WHOLESALE KILLING   75

CHAPTER 12: SOME COMMENTS ON CRIME AND THE SOCIETY   89

CHAPTER 13: HOW TO DESTROY A CIVILIZATION — OURS   97

CHAPTER 14: A GLANCE AT CHURCH REFORMERS IN LATIN
AMERICA   99

CHAPTER 15: AMERICAN LEMMINGS ON THE MARCH   103

CHAPTER 16: A PROBATION REPORT IS BASED ON AVAILABLE
RECORDS AND HEARSAY...   105

CHAPTER 17: MORE THAN THE MIND CAN BEAR   111

CHAPTER 18: SOME COMMENTS ON WRITTEN AND ORAL
HISTORY   115

CHAPTER 19: OUR STORY: SOCIAL COMMENTS ON PAST
EMPIRES—AND CALIFORNIA   119

CHAPTER 20: OUT OF COLLEGE AND INTO THE WORK FORCE   125

CHAPTER 21: DRIFTING TOWARD CIVIL WAR IN NORTH
AMERICA   129

CHAPTER 22: SUMMARY: WHAT HAPPENED TO THE
UNITED STATES?   157

CHAPTER 24: ON TREACHERY   159

CHAPTER 25: THE WAY IT IS TODAY   165

READING   169

ENDNOTES   170

INTRODUCTION

I drove by a brick warehouse that was built when the town was first formed, along the side of a railroad track. Like many towns, Oakdale was founded next to a reliable water supply — a river, the Stanislaus River. From a distance, the building looked fine, but as I got closer I could see that a portion of the wall had caved in.

As I drove by, I saw that one window casing was missing some bricks. It was a sure indication that the structure was no longer sound and would someday fall down. It would no longer be of use for the people who built it or for those who had used it in the past. The shadowy figures of some workers could be seen inside the building, and for a moment I thought about the safety issue and concluded that they must surely know about the dangerous circumstances they were in. That building will fall down someday, but no one can say how soon. Perhaps the workers inside were removing what was salvageable before they demolished a structure that had once served human needs.

As a man with more past than future, I see similar signs in the world around us today. The foundations of American institutions will not hold up 'the walls' for much longer. With the stresses assailing our society, the government and economic system are likely to not only fall down but kill millions of Americans *and* members of other societies.

My views about the future of America will seem unacceptable to many readers; indeed, they are unacceptable to my own dreams. Jimmy Carter spoke of a malaise and invited people to the White House to discuss what it was that was making this society sick. The next Presidential candidate, a Hollywood actor and former employee of General Electric (and the du Pont family) — Ronald Reagan — offered America smiles and optimism in a time of tumult. The people voted for optimism and put the nation into the hands of people who gave us wars in Granada, Panama, and the two Gulf Wars. I do not offer optimism in this book. I am going to tell you why: someday, Americans will be killing Americans again.

It is my contention that the cabal that rules our society created a warfare state to supplant the welfare state. At the heart of the United States Constitution was, and is, the promotion of general welfare. It says we rebelled and formed a government to promote the general welfare. It did not say that the government was formed to promote aggression by our richest elite against the people of our country and the rest of the world.

In the course of a lifetime of reading, study, writing and reflection, I have had to confront many aspects of history that are not often laid bare for the eye to see, events and actions that are veiled behind righteous-sounding motives and rationales that deflect blame and focus our attention away from those whose interests were promoted to the destruction of others.

Such study leads one to the dismal conclusion that this society is headed toward more wars. The social conflicts are growing and will eventually blow up. Yes, I predict we will have another Civil War. Why? The goals of the neo-conservative social-economic movement are in conflict with the values and aspirations of the majority of US citizens; our society is being polarized. Corruption in business and government has eroded this civilization and the social problems may be systemic.

The society that lies eventually dies. Most people know that torturing and killing prisoners of war is an atavistic practice that sets our civilization back hundreds of years. The American people really do believe in personal freedom and their Bill of Rights. The Patriot Act assaults the Bill of Rights.

Today the American people are not sovereign, and they have lost political control over their own lives. They never had decision-making power over the privately-owned economy. Neo-conservatives were always against big government that regulated the privately-owned economy and checked their power. Now that our industrial and banking elite have captured the government, they want to expand the Patriot Act to consolidate their social power. We just had two fraudulent presidential elections and the majority of adult citizens do realize the Congress does not represent them. They already know that special-interest government is not democratic.

Lobbyism killed the Republic. The repeated lies of corporations, and the lies of the government, will not have limitless success. Our dynastic power elite families have fallen victim to their own myths. They are not "the Best above all the Rest." The United States is not "the sole Super Power" nor were the German Nazis "Super Men."

When I was a child, we were taught that the planet had fifty-two countries on it. After World War I and World War II, the old empires were broken up and we now have well over a hundred nations out of those collapsed empires, with more small states being pried loose all the time. The US weakens anyone it can, splitting them up and gaining influence in the helpless pieces that are left. But this new form of empire-building and installation of puppet states in the Middle East and Central Asia will not get us far. Captain Mahan, McKinder, Karl Haushofer, and Zbigniew Brzezinski noted that whoever controlled the "Heartland" would dominate the world, but America's greatest moment is past. We have spent our fortune in wars and we gave away our industries. There is little foundation left to build on.

The Bible says, "The Truth will make you free." Well, a 'Skull and Bones' man like George H.W. Bush countered that quote by saying, "The truth will get you dead."

A former intelligence operative appointed by Richard Nixon as CIA Director, Bush may have been referring to "whistle-blowers." Today, Pentagon and governmental agents are leaking all over the internet. Historians have delved into this nations' past and have uncovered disturbing facts never revealed by the media (the media that were supposed to be the guardians of democ-

The neo-conservative movement can be seen as an anti-democratic effort to construct a corporate, privately-owned government. Attentive citizens here and all over the world are alarmed at current American foreign policies. Even some somnolent Republicans are having thoughts about the New World Order. These are uneasy thoughts.

I believe that the privately-owned (corporate) mainstream media is complicit in hiding vital information from the people. Public relations companies have plastered over the cracks in our social system. Propaganda ministries have been successful in misleading the nation. The view I share with you is not a happy one, and in fact it depresses me to read what I have written. My own illusions have been shattered by what I have learned.

The United States has created nuclear weapons, chemical weapons, bacteriological weapons, and now laser weapons that can cut your car in half from outer space. That awesome military power has led some neo-conservatives to believe that they can dominate the world and seize the resources of other countries. (The oil billionaires are the same families who have control over most of this nation's coal, natural gas, and uranium!) What were those elite families after, if not an energy monopoly? It is no accident of history that "Poppy" Bush, the Trust Fund Baby Bush, Donald Rumsfeld, and Condoleezza (Chevron) Rice all have a background, if fleeting, in the Oil business.

The economic power of elite families has been translated into political power. They now make decisions that affect our lives and deaths. As for the Christian-right true believers, what part of 'Thou shall not Steal, Lie or Kill' do they not understand? They just supported a predatory regime that lied about the WTC, lied about the Iraqi threat to us, and supported invading and stealing one whole country after another, with their valuable natural resources. Killing people that have not attacked us is immoral. Invading a country that is not attacking us is immoral ad it is a violation of the Treaty of Westphalia; it violates International law and has cost us allies and friends that we had for over two hundred years! The image of America as a shining example of the fresh new start for humankind has been tarnished, battered and fun over by the blind, monstrous ambition.

racy). In some cases, the truths they reveal are indeed getting whistle-blowers dead; in some cases, for putting US officials at risk for the crimes they committed; and in any case, for killing off the glorious illusion of what America stood for.

Over 50% of the populace no longer believe nor trust mainstream media outlets. In his day, Hitler had to burn books to control public opinion. In the US, Allen Dulles is known to have observed, "Americans don't read books."

Yet everything I write about is inspired by what I have read; 3,728 authors have provided me with the information and views which I share with you in this book. That being said, 38% of newspaper articles were designed by right-wing think-tanks to manipulate public opinion, that is, to "control your mind" and "influence elections." The same dynastic families that tried to install a fascist government in the United States (in 1933) fund those foundations and those think-tanks! They failed back then, but their spawn and minions succeeded in selecting Reagan and Bush. Heritage, CATO, American Enterprise Institute, and a hundred other organizations have their people in the White House and in government today.

As a Deputy Probation Officer, I worked for ten years with juvenile criminals. I learned early that family secrets hide tragic injuries that constitute crimes. National secrets, and national lies, are no different; they hide national crimes. War has always been mass murder and is always white-washed by propagandists. The American civilization has created the means to destroy itself with the creation of the warfare state. This is the bad news; we do not know what to do, because most of us do not know what has happened. The easiest solution is to not see any problems. The denial defense works for possums and ostriches, but not very well for the victims of deceit. I am no Cassandra warning the Trojans not to bring the wooden horse into the city; Washington has already fallen.

Machiavellian stealth politics have succeeded in controlling our "free and fair elections," as will be explained in later chapters. Patriotic Americans are disheartened to see that our own country does not live up to the ideals we preach around the world. We leave our children and grandchildren a Herculean task, which is to restore the influence of the American people on their government. The conflicts ahead will be greater than almost any this country has faced before.

A future economic crisis will be followed by a political conflict. This society is in a pre-revolutionary phase. In recent years, the approval rate for Congress fell to 15 % and even down to 10 %. Worldwide, other societies are also enduring harsh business cycles and political distress. Multiple coalition governments have been re-arranged specifically to meet economic crisis. Our mild-mannered Canadian neighbors were recently heard banging pots and pans in protest movements. In Mexico, the government is fighting drug cartels with a massive loss of life. What will the explosion look like here?

CHAPTER 1: THE DECLINE OF REPRESENTATIVE GOVERNMENT
IN THE UNITED STATES

A look at history books, or even Webster's Unabridged Dictionary, can be revealing. This country had sixteen Presidents until Lincoln was shot and killed. From 1776 until around 1865, we had around 76 years of leaders being left intact during their administrations. Elections, rather than assassinations, determined who would lead the people. Since that first political murder, this nation has had 141 years of intermittent violence directed at our presidents and presidential candidates. Factions have been subverting the Republic and practicing indirect elite rule. When this nation was an agrarian-based society, it was a lot safer to run for public office. After our industrial revolution, and the rise of 'Robber Barons,' our highest office became far more dangerous as new types of men translated their economic power into political power.

Our Civil War was based on many issues besides tariffs, including regionalism, slavery, and States Rights. The landed aristocracy of the South challenged the rising industrial leaders of the North, who were changing the rules of the game to their own great advantage; that conflict was the most devastating war in our history. The secessionist movement failed at great cost to a society that was undergoing constant change.

Let us examine what happened after Lincoln's assassination: James Garfield, President from March 1881–September 1881, was shot. President William McKinley, 1897–1901, was shot. President Theodore Roosevelt, 1901–1909 was shot but survived to challenge the power of big corporations with anti-trust laws and regulatory agencies to counter the power of privately-owned businesses that became monopolies. A 'Skull and Bones' man, Howard Taft, became president without getting shot. Wilson, Harding, Coolidge, and Herbert Hoover managed to serve out their terms without being shot. (There are suspicions that Harding died from poisoning, but his wife would not permit an autopsy and we will never know whether he too was assassinated.)

Franklin Delano Roosevelt was running for the highest office in the land when the nation was enduring the fifth year of the 'not so Great' Depression. A doctor's wife, Lilian Cross, changed the history of the United States with a motion of her hand. She saw an arm raised, holding a pistol aimed at the candidate. She pushed the arm of the assassin with these results: Anton Cermak, the Mayor of Chicago, was killed and four others were shot. However, Franklin Delano Roosevelt survived and was elected for four terms as a liberal president. He initiated the "New Deal"; Social Security; the Securities Exchange Commission; the Civil Conservation Corps; increased governmental regulation over the privately owned economy; and the Works Progress Administration (WPA) — a massive public works program giving jobs to the unemployed. He created welfare programs and used Keynes' theory of economic spending, by the government, to stimulate economic growth.

The industrial and banking elite hated Roosevelt and saw him as a "class traitor." They feared that these concessions, which cut into their profits, were only the beginning; they also feared that farmers and workers would revolt and take over the factories and create a Bolshevik State — as happened in 1917 in Russia. The American Liberty League was founded by 156 of our most powerful, and richest, families in 1933 to overthrow the elected government and install a fascist model state. The military would not go along with it and Congress covered up the plot to protect their sponsors.

Some of these same elite families supported the fascist movements in Europe in the 1930s. Henry Ford funded the American "Bund" Nazi party with rallies in Madison Square Garden in 1939. The elite families founded and funded underground American fascist organizations: "The Silver Shirts," the "Crusaders," "America First Committee," "Social Justice," "Sportsmen," and others. All these families and their subversive organizations went underground during World War II. You will hear more about them later. For now, we return to assassinations and the decline of democracy in the United States.

America stayed out of the shooting war long enough to be the last country standing. Roosevelt collected the victor's spoils in what is recorded as America's victory over the European fascist states. He died in office, having served for almost sixteen years.

Harry Truman, his Vice President, was subsequently elected and became our 33rd president. An assassination attempt was made by Puerto Rican separatists while Truman was living at Blair House in Washington D.C. A police officer and the assassins were killed during the attempt. Congressional representatives, too, were shot at another incident by Puerto Rican separatists.

The next President, Dwight D. Eisenhower, was not attacked in office. His Vice President, Richard Nixon, served as a liaison with the CIA for the 'Bay of Pigs,' the invasion of Cuba planned by Allen Dulles. However, John F. Kennedy won the election! Right-wing military me proposed shooting astronaut John Glenn down with a missile and blaming Cuba. That conspiracy was intended to prepare the public for war. This second Pentagon plan to use Cubans to kill Americans was also rejected, but it is an example of the kinds of "plans" that are used to shape events.

It is difficult to create fear and anger in the population unless they believe they are about to be attacked. John Kennedy refused to use the Navy to back up the Dulles plan when the invasion failed to gain support among the Cuban population. For this, he was deemed 'soft on communism' by our dynastic elite families.

JFK was assassinated in Dallas, Texas, and the number of conspiracy theories and distracting misinformation churned out since then have buried beyond hope any chance of ever learning exactly how it was done. On the day of his assassination, billionaire right-wing ideologues had placed an advertisement in the paper accusing President Kennedy of "treason." No one knew, at that time, that Prescott Bush had lost $53 million when Fidel Castro nationalized West Indies Sugar. Few knew that the anti-communist Dulles Brothers (John Foster Dulles and Allen Dulles) had both worked for the dynasty that had a financial interest in the United Fruit Company. President Kennedy had fired CIA Director, Allen Dulles, for his involvement in the "Bay of Pigs" invasion fiasco. Another 'Skull and Bones' man from Yale, Henry Luce (the media mogul), had interviewed Kennedy to make sure his foreign policy would remain anti-communist. Time Magazine held back the film by Abraham Zapruder to prevent the docile public, for decades, from seeing the evidence of conspiracy so that the legend of the "lone, crazed gunman" could be spun. Ever since, we have been spooked stories of lone, crazed gunmen, giving us the impression that nothing is safe. Even in schools, we welcome a pat down by armed guards.

One reason Kennedy got us into the Vietnam War was because of its resources in rubber, tin and potential oil deposits off the coast. The people were told this was a war for freedom and democracy.

The war was also supposed to hem in China and show that Kennedy was not, after all, soft on communism. Those aspects of communism that might sound good to the bottom 90% of society come at the cost of dispossessing the wealthy 10%. This kind of thinking will always be a threat to the owners of our economic system based on private property.

Anti-communism had been the cornerstone of American foreign policy since the Russian Revolution. Still, Kennedy was wary of getting drawn too far into a proxy war. He ordered a cutback of American support to South Vietnam on Thursday, November 21, 1963.[1] On Friday, November 22, 1963, he was dead. On Monday morning, November 25, 1963, the new president, Lyndon Johnson, canceled the withdrawal of advisors and escalated the war in Vietnam. The war profited the industrial military complex that President Eisenhower warned about in his farewell address.

Bobby Kennedy ran against Lyndon Johnson in the next election and was assassinated the night he won the California primary. He was leaning toward ending the war, after another democratic candidate (Eugene Mc Cathy) came out against continuing the war in South East Asia. A decade of slaughter was dividing the nation. 'Peaceniks' (opponents of war) were on the march in major cities.

Martin Luther King Jr., the national civil rights leader, was assassinated shortly after he came out against the Vietnamese war. He was preparing to run for the Presidency, supporting an anti-poverty platform — the kind of thing that smacks of "socialism" and scares the ones who prefer to squeeze the last drop out of working families.[2]

George Wallace, a Democratic presidential candidate, held some appeal among conservative Whites. But at the time, Nixon was counting on a "Southern strategy" to capture the votes of people who still preferred racial segregation — those whites who feared the Civil Rights Movement that benefited black citizens. Governor Wallace was shot on May 15, 1972, and was left permanently paralyzed from the waist down. That assassination attempt assured there would be no challenge to a Nixon presidency.

Nixon's regime ended in threatened impeachment, with more of his administration officials being sent to prison than any other regime in the nation's history.

Gerald Ford pardoned the Nixon crimes and he paid for that by losing the next election. The elite wanted Ford out so they could put Nelson Rockefeller in power; they knew the people would elect a Democrat.

President Ford chose to run, and the elite decided to kill him. A former hit man for J. Edgar Hoover refused the "contract"; this was an insider's plot. Amateurs were recruited for the assassination.[3] Perhaps Gerald Ford did not know that Bob Lovett — a 'Skull and Bones' man — had designed the highly secret, compartmentalized CIA. The Church Committee in Congress discovered that the Central Intelligence Agency was functioning like "Murder Inc.," and were overthrowing governments in other countries and engaging in assassinations. President Ford tried to stop the agency from violating our own laws and international law. Shortly after that, "Squeaky Fromme," a former Charles Manson follower, tried to shoot President Ford at William Land Park in Sacramento, California. After that failure, a second attempt on President Ford's life was carried out by another "lone, crazed gunwoman" in San Francisco as he was entering the St. Francis Hotel. (A former hit man and author — who was given as a gift to J. Edgar Hoover by Frank Costello — said he was offered the "contract" on Gerald Ford but declined). He was in Dallas, the day after the assassination, to dispose of the man who shot at Governor John Connolly.

Mainstream media ignores some books for what they reveal. In all probability, the Jack Kennedy assassination was not solved because members of both political parties were complicit, as well as the sponsors of Lyndon Baines Johnson and Richard Milhous Nixon. This could not have happened without the complicity of mainstream media. Dorothy Killgallen was the only reporter that saw Oswald alone in the judge's chambers, and she said to colleagues, "I'm going to blow this case wide open." Later she died suspiciously of a drug and alcohol overdose. We'll never know what it was she had found out.

The following is a digression: Sometimes planes and helicopters fall out of the sky. "Dictator" Omar Torrijos ruled Panama from 1968 to 1981; he instituted major public works, built schools, and negotiated for the Panama Canal to be turned over to Panamanian control. He had an air accident. "Dictator" Manuel Noriega, a CIA asset, assumed power. Later, he too was removed by an American invasion to retain control of the Panama Canal. Noriega wanted more than he was getting from the Bush–Reagan administrations, and he threatened to blackmail a 'Skull and Bones' man.

One might ask, were the air crashes of Lockerbie and those that killed Ron Brown (the first African-American Secretary of Commerce), Senator Carnahan, Senator Paul Wellstone, and John Kennedy Jr. all accidents? Wellstone's death shifted power to the Republicans in the Senate until Senator Jeffords switched parties over environmental and social issues.

Some at Scotland Yard say that the CIA planted evidence to indicate that it was Libyan intelligence agents who planned the bombing. Another source indicated that six CIA agents died at

Lockerbie. Rumor has it that they were going to reveal CIA mal-feasance. (Lt. Commander Al Martin, Naval Intelligence Officer and scam artist for the CIA, revealed that Criminals in Action (CIA) have assassinated over 243 US government agents, military, etc.)

Ronald Reagan beat 'Skull and Bones' man George H. W. Bush in the Republican primaries for the presidency. About two months into the Reagan presidency, Neil Bush (brother of George W. Bush) had to cancel his dinner engagement with the Hinckley Family. Why? Because it was the Hinckley boy who shot White House Press Secretary James Brady and put an explosive bullet two inches from President Ronald Reagan's heart. The Media failed, in this situation, as only John Chancellor of NBC mentioned the dinner plans[4] before the public relations companies and major media worked their propaganda, entertainment, and distractions — and killed that part of the story.

The 'Skull and Bones' society came to Yale University from Germany in 1832. The parent organization was called the "Thule Society," a secret Order known as the "Brotherhood of Death." General William Huntington Russell and Alphonso Taft founded the order with 15 tapped members per year. Howard Taft was the first 'Bones man' to become president. There are about 600 living 'Bonesmen' at any one time.

There is a difference between a fraternity and an intergenerational social power network. It may be just a coincidence of political history that the number of assassinations has increased with the industrial revolution and the rise of the Robber Barons that translated their economic power into political power. We had 76 years of relative social peace before Lincoln was shot. Since then we have had open season on presidents and presidential candidates. Populist candidates, who want to represent the populace, do not receive financing from elite dynastic families. A government formed by the majority of eligible voters has no chance because the centralized major media was founded and funded by a cabal that ignores candidates other than those of their own choosing. Two fraudulent elections and black box voting machines have not restored public confidence in the flawed electoral process. 'Bones man' John Kerry, and 'Bones man' George W. Bush, offered no real choice in the 2004 selection. Neither one would have pulled US troops out of Afghanistan and Iraq. No peace candidate was offered.

My e-mail from Tom Flocco, author of *Who Killed John-John*, says that John-John Kennedy was going to use his publication *George* Magazine for articles about the people who had killed his father, President John F. Kennedy. It asserts that John-John told his friends he was going to run for the Democratic nomination against Hillary Clinton and George W. Bush, the Republican candidate. Reportedly, a cut-off Mossad agent planted C-4 with a barometric device on John-John's plane that blew it out of the sky and over the ocean so it would look like an accident. This information was sent to 300 media outlets that continue to ignore it to this day. One media source reportedly said, "We don't want to topple the government!" Laurance Rockefeller (deceased) and the teleconferenced "Council of Thirteen" were in the Oval Office along with: "Poppy" Bush and his son Governor Bush, Hillary and Bill Clinton, Louis Freeh, and Attorney General Janet Reno. Witnesses have reportedly already testified about the plotters to a Federal Grand Jury that indicted L. "Scooter" Libby, the former White House Chief of Staff for Dick Cheney.

Patrick Fitzgerald is the Federal Prosecutor who deals with current crimes committed in the White House. Leaders of both major parties were involved in political assassinations. If this e-mail is factual, it means that three presidents and a current United States Senator are felons. The presence of Laurance Rockefeller, and the participation of the "Council of Thirteen," should shred some illusions about the part the dynastic power elite have played in this nation's tragic history. This elite, who sponsor candidates, have broken the social compact between the rulers and the ruled. National secrets have hidden national crimes, and recent governments have not been legitimate or concerned about the populace — other than to conceal their crimes. The privately owned media is complicit.

Factions that compete for public office by murdering rivals are not good guarantors of social peace. In fact, assassinations have only led to more assassinations. Sane societies are based on rational cooperation, not deadly competition. Societies are held together by rules, and laws, that have been agreed upon. Those that break those rules or laws threaten the entire social structure. Once a group decides that they have a right to kill their rivals for reasons of power, they are laying the groundwork for their own annihilation.

Our men and women in Iraq and Afghanistan cannot distinguish their friends from their enemies. That means many innocent people are killed. If we have another civil war in our future, US citizens will be put in the same position of trying to identify those who support democracy from those who have worked to install a corporate or fascist state.

As our society is being polarized by the neo-conservatives on the one hand and those who ramp up the flames of identity politics on the other. Little thought is given to the notion of building on common interests, such as a strong economy, instead of digging a deeper trench of separation. At this rate, both sides are accelerating the drive to a new civil war. Neo-conservatives who thought politics was another form of warfare will be the likely victims of that worldview.

Those who believe in the social thought espoused by Thomas Hobbes may become victims of the belief that life is nasty, brutish, and short. Few realize that social war began already with the attack on the World Trade Center and the Pentagon. That self-inflicted wound was followed up by the panic-inducing delivery of anthrax powder from our own laboratories to Congress (who could have had the access, and the cynicism, to do that?), and the assault on our civil liberties by the Patriot Act.

Some know, and many more suspect, that the Bush-Cheney administration had a hand in the attack on WTC or at least allowed it to happen in order to justify the invasion of Iraq. Iraq never attacked the WTC. The first so-called attack by Islamic militants was carried out by people who were trained by the American government to blow things up. Britain and the United States trained and funded the Mujahedeen to throw the Soviets out of Afghanistan. Then they were proclaimed as "Our" freedom fighters against communism. Later they became our terrorists that blew up Khobar Towers, the USS Cole in Yemen, and then two of our embassies in Africa.

There is no rational explanation for how some of the men named as WTC hi-jackers were discovered alive and well in the Middle East. Some of them were trained to fly in US military installations. Osama bin Laden was a CIA asset when he fought the Soviets in Afghanistan. We provided the religious fanatics with stinger missiles to shoot down communist planes and helicopters. Pakistani intelligence was the go-between or cut off. Arab money from Wahhabis, and American taxpayers' money, built the terrorist training camps and funded the intrusion into Afghanistan as another proxy war against America's communist rivals.

The American elite families are very insecure about democratic elections that threaten their economic power. Taxes and governmental regulation of corporations are the bane of their existence. That is why we had two fraudulent elections with rigged voting machines, after a candidate selection process that practically eliminates any non-corporate candidates anyway. The dynastic power want to privatize the government even more; and they are against Big Government unless they own it with sponsored candidates and minions.

The historical trend is obvious; we are in an age of assassinations and wars. The social myth is that we are a democracy and that the people's will is implemented by elections, yet the reality is otherwise. Gun-ocracy has replaced democracy, when necessary. Indeed, there is no need to kill when the dynastic power elite elects the favored candidate.

Bob Lovett, a 'Skull and Bones' man, designed the CIA, which has engaged in "Black operations" all over the globe. That shadow governmental agency has been violating our US laws and international law. Torturing and killing prisoners of war are just the tip of an iceberg. That agency has also killed foreign leaders and political targets. General "Wild Bill" Donovan was a former Wall Street lawyer who thought the OSS, which later became the CIA, was ideal for performing black operations all over the globe, and "wet operations," otherwise known as murder. Frank Wisner (CIA) said, "Everybody does it," — he was referring to assassination. There is nothing democratic or patriotic in murdering our own or foreign citizens, or our own agents.

Jimmy Carter, an honest man by any account (a quality that may make it hard to serve as president) was vaguely aware of the malaise that affected our society. He had Admiral Stansfield

Turner fire hundreds of CIA agents; however, most of them were rehired to work for organizations connected to 'Bones man" "Poppy" Bush, the former CIA Agent, Director of CIA, and President. Others went to work for corporations. I believe that Jimmy carter was chosen by the Rockefellers to replace the dishonest President Nixon who had tarnished the institution. But presidents like Carter, and perhaps most of the others, could not and cannot control all branches of the government. The CIA was still doing bad things to people in Latin America during the Carter years.

Corruption, immorality and illegality are always a great hazard in any government. They may infect government institutions from Day One. The war for independence was our first civil war against England and the Tories, intended in part to fight back against their corruption. The next chapters will describe some of the factors today that are leading this society to another civil war, which our children and grandchildren will fight.

The nation has forgotten the attempt on President Andrew Jackson's life, when he opposed the penetration of our banking system by the Rothschild dynasty; he accused them of the attempt. The Rothschilds' agents offered loans at 26% interest to Lincoln, who declined, and later offered interest rates of 16%. Instead, Lincoln had the government print a new currency called "Greenbacks," that were not tied to the gold reserves in the bank. This was a deadly real threat to big bankers: the corporate bankers and the wealthy families whose fortunes are intertwined with them, the "financiers." Lincoln was killed not only, and probably not mostly, over slavery. Freeing the currency from the control of a central bank made him more dangerous enemies than freeing the slaves had done.

Much later, realizing a bit too late what the game was, President Wilson exclaimed, "I just ruined the country." He was referring to the Federal Reserve Act that was passed in 1913, and he was right.

CHAPTER 2: THE SECRET ORDER CAME FROM GERMANY IN 1832

Skull and Bones — The Secret Order: Social Impact

Skull and Bones is nominally a private organization that inducts seniors at Yale University (by invitation) as members — lifetime members. Although its membership list is public, much of its activities, and its aims, are secret. "Bonesmen" from Yale started the following organizations: American Historical Association, American Psychological Association, American Economic Association, Planned Parenthood, American Medical Association, American Chemical Society, American Civil Liberties Union, American Peace Society. Bones members also control these major foundations: Carnegie, Ford, Peabody, Slater, and Russell Sage, etc.

The Order appears to concentrate on how to change society toward a specific goal: a "New World Order." They have been Hegelians, often supporting opposing social movements so that they always control the discourse and so control the outcomes. Thesis versus anti-thesis eventuates in a synthesis.

This organization came from Germany and was influenced by the social thought processes of Hegel and Nietzsche. They were interested in creating super men; and they hedged their bets. Historically, they supported both sides of social movements.

These and other organizations have had a tremendous impact on our society. That includes Bob Lovett, Bonesman, who designed our shadow government — the Central Intelligence Agency! That is a small inkling of the influence they have had on American society. They have far more power than indicated by the mentioned organizations, especially when they are in government. They have had impact on foreign policies and our financial institutions. Their members are involved in Law, the CIA, Education, the Media, (e.g. Henry Luce was a Bonesman). They have launched or penetrated foundation think-tanks, legislatures, Federal Reserve Systems, businesses, and some Churches. They are highly secretive because they have to be.

This secret order has been operating in the US since 1832. Howard Taft was the first Bonesman to be US President. The secret order are an intergenerational social power network; they promote and protect each other; they constitute a secret real "Establishment." They were known as the "Brotherhood of Death" in Germany; they lived up to their name. Take a look at their history, a history that goes back to the 1700's. There are around 600 living Bonesmen at this time in our history. Both Bush Presidents were Bonesmen. Senators John Kerry and Boren from Oklahoma, on the Intelligence Oversight Committee, are also Skull and Bonesmen. Prescott Bush, George Herbert Walker, the Harriman brothers, and the Brown brothers, all came from that secret order. They mutually support and protect each other.

Alphonso Taft founded the single American branch. Another Chapter went to Oxford and All Souls College. They changed their name to the innocuous-sounding, "The Group." In America, the secret order changed their name again to the Order of "Skull and Bones." Fifteen seniors a year are admitted to this elite group.

This is a social power network that has a historical past. Back in imperial Austria, baggage fell off a carriage and what was found there revealed the secret plans of the "Illuminati" to overthrow the monarchy and aristocracy, and to dominate the world. The Illuminati were anti-clerical Republicans persecuted by the police. They fled to Germany and changed their name to the "Thule Society." An American general brought them from Germany to Yale. His name was William Huntington Russell. (His family fortune was founded on the opium trade; later, the CIA went into the drug business when OSS discovered Chiang Kai Chek was running his whole warlord army on the opium trade);

It cost millions of lives in World War One to rid Europe of fifty-four monarchs and the aristocracy. The goal was achieved: to destroy the Old World political systems, empires, and aristocracies founded on hereditary rights. They were also anti-clerical in France.

This is significant: Bob Lovett, Skull and Bones man, designed the CIA. It is a highly compartmentalized, and secret, agency that acts as a shadow government and controls or overthrows governments in the US and abroad. They also assassinate — "accidents," "natural causes" and "suicides" are their specialty.*

Henry Luce, a Skull and Bones man, was a media mogul for *Time* and *Life* magazines and created a media empire that now includes movies and TV major news media.

Here are examples of other dynastic power-elite families that have had membership within the Skull and Bones secret order: Buckley, Samuel Bush (during World War I and II), the Harriman Brothers (robber barons; Central American secret, dirty wars funded by CIA cocaine deals, Panama, Grenada, Gulf War, Afghanistan and Iraq war); Brown Brothers (Brown Shirts); George Herbert Walker and Prescott Bush (Hitler project); H.L Stimson (World War II), the Bundy brothers (Vietnam War); Lovett (Cold War); Percy Rockefeller (related to John D. Rockefeller — eugenics movement, population control projects); Cheney, Dodge, Pillsbury, Vanderbilt, Taft, Weyerhaeuser and Whitney.

These are just a few of the dynastic families that practice effective indirect rule because they own the private economy. Some of the elite are Hegelians that fund opposing sides of social movements; they support both sides of a conflict so they will

---

* Read *The Conspirators* by Lt. Commander Al Martin, a former Naval Intelligence Officer who worked for the CIA for 14 years, involved in scams including Iran-Contra and other Bush family crimes.

always win and have influence. They never lose a conflict in the synthesis.

For example, Samuel Bush supplied arms for the Kaiser of Germany in World War One. He profited from both sides because he was on the War Production Board and supplied Remington and Thompson arms to the United States Army. He also provided arms to the Nazi Party in the 1930s.

Some du Pont family members demonstrated how "thesis versus anti-thesis equals synthesis" when they utilized the Democratic Leadership Council to support the Al Gore and Joseph Lieberman Campaign in 2004. Big donations eliminated populist candidates who received less funding and were ignored by the media. At the same time, du Pont interests funded the right-wing think-tank members who became the neo-conservative members of the government today. Yes, they funded Cheney and Bush too. They could afford to buy both parties! They would not lose influence.

Corporations are the economic arms of our dynastic elite families. Only the American people lost influence. This could be one reason so few eligible voters usually bother to vote.

Skull and Bones members have great secrets as they establish "The New World Order." Both Presidents Bush plus John Kerry are Bonesmen. This alone means that the American people never had a chance for peace. There are "Bonesmen" in Congress, including Senator Boren from Oklahoma, Senator John Kerry, and many others.

All were dynastic families that formed League in 1933. They tried to get General Darlington Smedley Butler to overthrow the government and establish fascism. They planned on using the American Legion and Van Zandt of the V.F.W.

Veterans should know some of this history. Most citizens do not. We tend to be oblivious as to the social history of the dynastic power elite families. Neo-conservatives are not traditional Republicans; they have a deadly racist past. In *The War Against the Weak*, Edwin Black describes "The campaign to create a 'master race' in the United States." Adolf Hitler wrote to one of our Eugenics organizations thanking them for their research. The elites also funded the concept of 'planned parenthood,' enforced sterilization projects, and founded the American Psychological

Association (They were always interested in controlling other people's minds, and still are). Regarding the American Historical Association, they believe you can control the past by controlling how we describe it and then control the future.

In case you have not guessed it by now, it took over two hundred years of evolution for the German "Thule Society" to become the Nazi political party.

In America, that single chapter of the Thule Society changed their name to "Skull and Bones." I will wager that you do not know what was on the caps, and on the lapels, of every German SS guard in the death camps, and on the uniforms of the Waffen SS.

"The truth will get you dead." Our former CIA Director, Ambassador to the U.N., Vice President, and President was/is also a business partner of the Bin Laden family (Carlyle Group) and also a business partner to the Hinckley family. "I don't like to kill police officers . . . unless it is absolutely necessary," as CIA Director William Casey once said. He, too, is deceased — having been diagnosed with a brain tumor.

So far, over one hundred cameramen and news people have been killed in Afghanistan and Iraq.

Did you know that Prescott Bush lost $53 million in the West Indies sugar industry when Fidel Castro nationalized the family holdings? Could that have had any connection to the "Bay of Pigs" invasion and "Cuban Missile Crisis"? Where was "Poppy" Bush at that time? The Dulles Brothers both worked as attorneys for the United Fruit Company. Both also negotiated a reduction of reparations payments to Nazi Germany. Their clients had joint ventures with Nazi companies. Allen Dulles was the CIA director when Kennedy fired him. The Bush dynasty invested in the United Fruit Company. (The du Ponts and Rockefellers also have interests in Latin American countries). This should give you an idea of which team each one was playing on.

The CIA killed a reporter in Florida because he would not surrender his pictures of US military equipment in the camp of the Cuban invasion operation; he was run off the road by a van and his story disappeared. The earlier attempt to buy him off had failed in a Florida hotel room, and he tried to get back to New York.

The agency had penetrated the media and knew about his reporting of the impending intervention in Cuba. Katherine Graham's husband, publisher of the Washington Post, was an intelligence operator as were some other Washington Post reporters. They kept quiet about this story and protected the Yale Skull and Bonesmen regarding the "Bay of Pigs" fiasco.

Operation "Mockingbird" was a secret campaign by the CIA to influence the media, using informants and agents.

Regarding organizations started by Bonesmen: If you can control history textbooks, you can influence the future. Increased understanding of psychology could lead to improved methods of influence, of mind control and social control activities. Bonesmen already have social power over the economy and law institutions. The institutions through which they project influence usually support private property rights over human rights. Their interest in health, education, and the media may look like they are concerned with the good of humanity, but details give away the subterranean goal of preserving elitism — the welfare of their own dynastic families. Members of the secret order call themselves "the best above all the rest."

The US now has genocidal weapons at their disposal (anthrax, smallpox and other deadly microbes). Congress panicked when anthrax from US laboratories was sent to them by mail. And they passed the Patriot Act so fast that no one on their staff could have read even half of it.

Some of these elites have been Social Darwinists and supported the Eugenics movement in Germany, United Kingdom, and the United States. Thirty-seven states had eugenics laws before the Nazis embarked on their campaign to eradicate the so-called weak and "unfit." Did they feel any compunction? Frank Wisner, a CIA agent, said, "Everybody does it" (assassinate and murder). The Illuminati, Thule Society, Skull and Bones, is in fact a secret *criminal* society. Historically they have been supra legal — after all, they are Nietzschean "Super Men"! Their dynastic families profited from human conflict. Skull and Bonesmen are predators.

The neo-conservative movement is taking this society on a death march. We face expanding wars in an age of great risk. The internal troubles in Pakistan are a direct result of American foreign policies. A right-wing historian, Samuel Huntington, predicted a clash between Western Civilizations and Islamic societies. I believe that more than a clash in spiritual values is involved. Our current imperialism is based on the economic and political goals of our dynastic elite families. Their past success has led to today's conflicts.

Our rice bowl, our lives, and the future of this society are not being protected against the neo-conservative social movement. Ignorance is not bliss; in this age it is dangerous. Remington guns and Olin bullets were used in the coup attempt of 1933, by the unemployed "bonus" marchers. Samuel Bush had interests in Remington Arms. Their arms have been killing for generations. They, and the du Ponts, have been "Merchants of Death."

Chapter 3: Where Did the American Fascist Families of the 1930s Go?

Fascism was created to serve as a check on the Bolshevik Revolution, a revolution that had, in itself, been created to destroy Russia before it could conceivably develop into a potential rival. Winston Churchill was one of the very first to note, about Bolshevism: "We will strangle that baby in its crib." Didn't he know it was the West that funded Lenin and gave him a private train to slip back into Russia just before? Playing both sides.

The owners of private property in Britain, the United States, and in other capitalist countries sent troops into Russia. They aided the Whites, the Czar, and the Russian aristocracy whose power base was actually feudalism. The Western nations and the Czar lost the war, and the peasants and workers set up an autocratic state under Lenin and later Stalin. The Communist victory evolved into a totalitarian police state, deplorable as that may be. At the same time, they fast forwarded a few hundred years and changed an agricultural society into an industrial super-power capable of defending itself.

Russia freed its serfs before the US freed the slaves, but Russia had little history of liberty as we think of it. It had been an empire for centuries, and now it had been infiltrated by foreign agents and subversives of many types, and was struggling to recover from social upheaval on top of civil war on top of World

War I. The new Soviet secret police were vigilant and ruthless, with external enemies and enemies within. The socialist/communist program was regimentarian, marshaling resources, include human resources, to meet the overall goals of society. Individual rights took a distant second place.

Yet communism was the fastest growing social movement in the history of the world. It spread faster than Christianity; it took Christianity three hundred years to replace the Roman Empire in Europe. They overthrew what were seen as predatory rich people and invested in schools, industry, and food production for the general benefit. They built housing and transportation infrastructure. Struggling workers elsewhere thought it sounded pretty good.

Meanwhile, since the "Reds" were shooting capitalists, every capitalist on the planet felt he was under threat. The very idea of an alternate model was too dangerous to be permitted; a strong anti-communist movement developed in the West to make sure that no such program could catch on here.

The dynastic power elite of Britain and the United States funded Nazi fascism, from 1923 until 1942, through the Union Bank of New York. The owners of vast amounts of private property were very much threatened by the idea of social property, the notion that the nation state would own the means of production, distribution, commerce and exchange. The Brown Brothers, Harriman Brothers, Prescott Bush, and George Herbert Walker were banking partners with common interests and they funneled money to the Brown Shirts and Hitler's Nazi Party. Fritz Thyssen — a German industrialist — and German aristocrats backed Hitler, as they feared a communist takeover of Germany. This kind of people were no friends of democracy or the new German Weimar Republic. Furthermore, like Henry Ford, many of them despised the Jewish-dominated circles of financial capital, and they funded the Fascist Party in the United States during the Great Depression.

A devastating business cycle hit the United States in 1929. With the stock market crash, the society went into economic, and some mental, depression. Massive bank failures, bankrupt businesses, and closed factories threw millions of people out of work and into poverty. The privately owned economic system of capitalism worked well for the rich but devastated millions of Americans. The Depression became worst worldwide when nations set up trade barriers, trying to protect their own industries from competition; the Smoot Hawley tariff made the situation worse.

Over 25% of workers were unemployed when Roosevelt took office in 1933. They suffered from hunger and malnutrition, even if there were soup kitchens available here and there. Veterans of World War One had descended on Washington to demand their due. There was widespread turmoil. President Roosevelt instituted the New Deal to offer some jobs and support in the crisis. However, such practices smacked of "socialism," and any hint of softening the edges of strict capitalism hinted at reducing the privileges of the upper crust.

The richest and most powerful 156 families panicked; they feared a revolution against their interests. They gathered and plotted to overthrow the government and set up a fascist model emulating Italy, Germany, and the Grand Feux movement in France.

The "American Liberty League" was created in 1934. They contacted Van Zandt — head of the Veterans of Foreign Wars — and retired Marine Corps General Darlington Smedley Butler, to head a "putsch." The du Pont and Olin families would provide the Remington rifles and Olin Bullets to arm the bonus marchers who were camped out in Washington; they had marched across the country in protest of their unemployment. The newly elected President, Franklin D. Roosevelt, and Cordell Hull, were to be killed. The mayor of Chicago was killed.

General Butler revealed the plot to J. Edgar Hoover and he testified in Congressional hearings, which were inquiring into Nazi propaganda circulating in the United States. Van Zandt also testified regarding the plot, as the Wall Street financiers had also propositioned him to commit treason. Congress did not call a single witness from among the Liberty League members. Rather, Congress covered up the plot, probably because these same dynastic families sponsored their elections. The *Philadelphia Record* revealed the plot details due to the investigative efforts of Paul Comly French. The Republican Party begged the Liberty League not to endorse any of their candidates in future elections!

Franklin Roosevelt brought in a "Brain Trust" of university and college teachers and went ahead to implement the "New Deal" social welfare programs. He set up economic recovery programs, social security, Public Works programs, and used a graduated income tax to finance the government. He used Keynesian theories to stimulate the economy to provide jobs; he used government intervention to save the free enterprise system from the crippling business cycle. The public elected him four times for a total of sixteen years. The super-rich hated him and, through the press and radio, attacked him, his wife Eleanor, family members, and even his dog Fala. The dynastic power elite hated the graduated income tax and considered Roosevelt a "class traitor."

The American Nazi party gathered 19,000 true believers at Madison Square Garden in 1939. Where did they go during the World War II when we fought Nazi Germany, Fascist Italy, and Imperial Japan? They went underground. The Bush family had financial interests in Madison Square Garden, by the way.

You might wonder what happened to the one hundred and fifty six families who distrusted democracy. Well, some of them ensured their corporations' trade with the Axis Alliance during the World War II; some performed espionage against the United States — companies like I.T.T. and RCA.* Some spied for the Nazis in the United States and in Latin American companies; some owned factories in Germany, France, and North Africa. Henry Ford refused to build airplanes for Winston Churchill, yet he built over a third of the German military vehicles in plants located in Germany, France, and North Africa. Hitler awarded Ford with the Golden Eagle, not the Iron Cross. Ford sent Hitler 50,000 reichmarks every birthday during the war. This occurred while US citizens were dying. Some of our elites supported both sides, all for profit, regardless of who won the war.

General Motors built planes for America during the war. Meanwhile, the General Motors plants in Europe (Opel) manufactured the Me262 Jet fighter for our enemies; they had connections with Nazis. The Rockefeller-controlled Standard Oil

---

* Charles Higham's book *Trading with the Enemy* has details; Curt Gentry's book on J. Edgar Hoover, *The Man and his Secrets*, is shocking. It shows which corporations the dynastic power elite control. They are household names familiar to every American.

Corporation provided fuel for submarines which sank US ships and those of US allies. The Philadelphia Ball-and Roller Bearing Company sent its products to South America to be transshipped to neutral countries and end up in Focke-Wulf fighters and Tiger tanks. Some American banks had secret deals with Nazi banks, laundering funds stolen from conquered countries. Just business.

American corporate traitors traveled to Britain and Portugal to warn German agents of the Eighth Air Force plans to bomb the ball bearing facilities in Schweinfurt. The forewarned Germans were waiting and shot down 60 US planes. Ten men on each plane were killed, wounded, or captured. Rockefeller had alliances with the I.G. Farben Works in Germany where The Standard Oil Company utilized slave laborers in the production of fuel from coal. The labor camps were organized by the German SS.

The story gets a lot worse, I warn you. Hitler got his ideas for concentration camps from America's use of Indian reservations. And Hitler saw the world sit by when the Turks massacred the Armenians. He wanted a pure super race, and he wanted to eliminate inferior peoples, and he figured he could get away with it.

During the same time period, there were strong currents of racism and elitism in the United States, where programs were funded to sterilize black people along with crippled, the blind, the retarded, and the mentally ill. Hitler killed the weak before he embarked on his Empire and his New World Order. He received the Nuremberg Laws idea from the Carnegie Institute, and other eugenicists such as Davenport, the Rockefellers, Carnegie, the Harrimans, the Bush family, and Reynolds too.

The eugenics movement began at Yale in 1908 in order to create a super race by eliminating the blind, the retarded, the crippled, the infirm and generally inferior people. Gobeneau of France, Herbert Spencer, and William Graham Sumner, all from Yale, had the intellectual antecedents to influence the social Darwinists that came from the finest families to Ivy League colleges. Our industrial elite looked upon themselves as the most fit to survive. They were true believers in competition in business and looked upon themselves as naturally created to rule.

They applied this reasoning in business, as well. After all, it was they who put less efficient enterprises out of business or gobbling them up in corporate mergers. The entire swath of 105 American automobile companies were reduced to just 5 companies.

These capitalists were growing in power and influence. They already knew that the greatest fortunes and profits were made during war; peace was not as profitable. The original fortunes of the du Pont family were made in the war of 1812 against England. Guess which chemical company made gunpowder and explosives? They profited in every war. Some writers called them the "merchants of death."

These families founded and funded the following organizations: Heritage, CATO, Olin, American Enterprise Institute, Federalist Society, and the Project for the New American Century Taxpayers Union. The Sound Economy was also funded by the following right-wing families: Coors, Ford, Rockefeller, and the conservative foundations — involving up to a hundred right-wing organizations. These organizations believe in laissez-faire capitalism ('let them do whatever they want'); they are against government regulation and social security; they want a free rein to privatize electric companies and water systems owned by municipalities. Why should they be barred from making a profit on our basic needs? They already own our medical care, our banks and the prisons.

They knew that robots and automation would create unemployment problems. They exploited the drugs and entertainment businesses that fill people's time and sap their ambition to further their lives. They had their agencies experiment with mind control drugs. They experimented with information management and methods of social control. And they are still doing it.

They created the warfare state and they need you to continue to ingest the information coming out of their TV networks, magazines, radios, publishing houses, and textbook companies. You and your family have always been the target of their public relations companies. You are to be entertained, distracted, and under-informed about crucial social issues. I believe there is no other society today that is the subject of such a massive propaganda drive as we are.

The spawn of the American Liberty League have their chosen representatives embedded in the White House, Congress, the Supreme Court, intelligence agencies, corporations, academia and the media. They call themselves neo-conservatives; even the Republicans do not recognize where they came from and what they want. They want to practice economic Imperialism.

They want our 6% of the world's population to be able to continue consuming 50% of the planet's energy; they plan to continue to dominate the world, even though we have lost the momentum that got us here. Our dynastic power elite are the wealthiest people in human history. They are abusing their economic power and that is why other nations fear and hate us.

We have our battle fleets in every ocean and troops in over forty countries. We have the weapons of mass destruction that endanger civilizations. One percent of our population owns 40% of all this nation's wealth, and they control private pension funds of millions of workers. The dynastic power elite denies they even exist, as they perpetuate the myth that we are a republic and have a democratic system of government.

We have evolved into a plutocracy where big money determines elections. It is lobbyism that has killed the Republic. Most Americans now know they do not have representation in Congress. It is only the special interests that are well represented. The rich sponsor their candidates; many congress people have clients, not constituents. There are exceptions; some try to represent the people. It is possible to find people in Congress who are honest and sincere, but notice the gridlock.

The du Ponts and General Electric funded the Democratic Leadership Council (Gore and Lieberman), and the Bush selection, in the last "selection." They also supported Bush. They hedged their bets. The du Ponts and General Electric created the trust foundations that have their personnel in government today. The trust fund babies have accomplished the goals of the Liberty League families; they could not have done this without the influence of the media.

Millions of Americans do not vote today because there is little difference between the two major parties; and the specific candidates put up for our vote are often personally repugnant anyway. Apathy is the friend of the status quo. Current foreign policies are dangerous to world peace but few Americans these days are protesting that. Identity politics has everyone demonstrating on personal grounds. The media has not guarded democracy very well.

The vested interests have already passed a law providing that the taxpayers will insure any American company against losses in Iraq and Afghanistan. That guarantees them continual profit. The money to fight these natural gas and oil wars was borrowed from banks. The payback was supposed to come from winning the wars, destroying those nations, and seizing their assets. It doesn't look too promising.

The American taxpayers are totally funding this dangerous war policy. Welcome to the new world order where the Patriot Act attack your civil liberties.

The people favor a democracy and their Bill of Rights. When they are aroused from their sleep, they will eventually resist business-ocracy. After all, they are workers who created this complex society. This nation holds liberal values in spite of the angry talking heads and apologists for unregulated capitalism. The people have always favored an equal opportunity society and they resent privilege. Trust funds, foundations, public relations companies and lobbyism have consolidated the social power of our dynastic elite families. The majority of the public are unaware, are programmed, and are manipulated by a media that is controlled by "private interests." The economically privileged determine the quality of our lives. Without concerted action, the populace is powerless.

Meanwhile the sheeple are oblivious. The warfare state has replaced the welfare state of the Roosevelt era. Islamic countries are resisting the establishment of American bases in the Middle East — that is, foreign occupation — while they are fighting a religious war. We fight an economic and political war with great technology, and we lose our friends as we make new enemies. Our industrial nation knows that there are limited supplies of natural gas and oil that all industrial nations require. The question is — will the other nations accept our domination?

Military conscription may eventually come back as we have several hundred thousand troops in Iraq, Kuwait and Afghanistan and some based in Central Asia, surrounded by a billion Moslems from Morocco to Indonesia. There are suicide bombers in our future. This nation will bleed for years yet still borrow the money to fight the so-called war on terrorism. Every time we kill, we make enemies of all his or her relatives. We should not be surprised.

Our CIA has been dealing drugs ever since we found out that Chiang Kai-shek had managed to fund his whole Kuomintang Army on opium. Colby shipped heroin into the United States in body bags. William Casey and "Ollie" North smuggled cocaine when Bush Sr. was Vice President. The CIA killed hundreds of members of our own government to cover up malfeasance. Janet Reno imprisoned over a thousand people to hide Agency crime. Today, the heroin is being harvested in Afghanistan, while the cocaine still comes up from South America.

The war on drugs is a war on *other drug operations, ones that compete with the CIA.*

Drugs are one of the most profitable businesses on the planet. Drug money was laundered and found its way into major banks.

Currently, those banks and foreign states that have loaned the US money to fight this war will make great profits. The dynastic families need an ample return on their investment. The media does not tell the public enough to protect them from the neo-conservative social movement. Even the Republicans do not know the historical background of the self-described neo-cons.

Chapter 4: Why Did the Media Fail to Protect the People?

Few Americans took note when an oil company buying up a movie company. Probably even less took notice when a tire company purchased a newspaper and TV company. Over the decades, powerful industrial organizations have acquired publishing houses, radio stations, magazines, and other media.

Americans are the most targeted people on the planet for advertisements. We are subject to around five thousand advertisements a day on billboards and radio, and are also subject to intrusive phone calls to our homes. Many companies buy out smaller companies and become conglomerates. The Hearst family operates approximately three hundred magazines. Public opinion is important and that is why billions of dollars are spent, by the dynastic power elite, to manipulate the minds of citizens.

In addition, there is a whole industry designed to manage social thought in the United States; it is called the public relations sector. It was constructed to make people think well of businesses, even as private interests took more power over people's lives. Public relations is one big economic propaganda ministry.

They are well-financed institutions that hide illegal and unethical programs of corporations. They cover up scandal, they white wash, spin, spread dis-informative half-truths, and create illusions for the unwary. The elite own, and operate, the private economy; the only other institution that could possibly challenge them is the Federal government. But they fund electoral campaigns so politicians listen to them.

That is why the real power brokers finance elements in both major political parties. They hedge their bets on who is to be a political leader. For example, the du Pont family funded the Democratic Leadership Council who ensured that Gore and Lieberman would run against their selected candidate, Bush. The du Pont interests also funded the right-wing foundations that formed the Bush government with loyal personnel. It did not matter to them who really won the election, but it does matter to the public as they are not represented. The selected government will be taking the calls of the lobbyist for General Electric and General Motors, or some other economic entity, which are owned by the real rulers.

Many politicians are representatives of special interests. That is why the social problems of the nation are ignored. Banks, insurance companies, war industries, drug companies, and industrial enterprises, are all well represented while common people are not.

The super wealthy have been running this country for a long time; it was probably during the Jackson presidency that most people had a powerful influence on the society. At that time, most of us were independent farmers in an Agrarian society. The Civil War, and the Industrial Revolution, created the great fortunes of our robber barons.

In the 20th century, big money, sponsored candidates, media control, and lobbyism, all had a part in dis-enfranchising the American people. The press gave no warning to the public as the oil interests gained control of the nation's coal supply. Society did not notice that the uranium for power plants, and nuclear weapons, came under the control of the same families that controlled vast energy sources in an industrial society.

The dynastic power elite rule indirectly through their corporations, trust foundations, public relations companies, newspaper chains, lobbyists, and sponsored candidates. Of course, they would deny that they have power, in order to perpetuate the myth that the United States is run as a democracy. We are no longer a Republic, even though two major political parties carry those names: Republicans and Democrats. We are a true plutocracy being run by an oligarchy.

Lies from the presidency are nothing new. President Wilson did it when he said, "We will make the world safe for Democracy" during World War I. President Kennedy lied at first about this nation's involvement in the Bay of Pigs invasion of Cuba. President Johnson lied about the Gulf of Tonkin resolution to get us into an expanded war in Vietnam.

President Nixon's lies got more of his administration into federal prisons than any other administration in history. President Bush Sr., and President Clinton, lied about the CIA bringing drugs into the United States to fund the war in Latin America against the Reds.

The biggest national secret of all is this: The United States Government is saturated by minions of the same foundations which were established by the one hundred and fifty six families of the "American Liberty League." These are the owners of corporations that continued to do business with the Nazis during the World War II. Some gave information and patents to Hitler, and they escaped confiscation and prosecution thanks to the media.

How do you recognize a Neo Con? Neo Cons are ardent anticommunists. They believe that socialism is communism. They hate and fear liberals because they do not want to see a Teddy Roosevelt or a Teddy Kennedy curtailing the power of corporations they control. They do not want another liberal administration to start any more cockamamie "Safety Net" programs at their expense, or tighten up the loopholes that allow corporations to evade paying taxes.

Karl Rove promised one hundred years of Republican rule. Even most Republicans do not know the nature of the powers behind the throne; private property is sacred to them. They want to own the world's resources and that is why we are in Iraq and Afghanistan and Syria. It is no historical accident that Cheney, Bush, and Bush Sr. were in the oil business; they were funded by that special interest. The oil people are the richest people on the planet and are all-powerful.

The neo-cons risk more than our troops in Asia and the Middle East. They rely on our fear of fundamentalist terrorists; they are fearful and insecure in the face of the current economic crisis, which will get worse. If we start to become immune to the "terrorist threat," they drum up a totally fictitious notion of "Russian aggression." They will invent outside enemies to unite us in fighting to maintain their own privileged positions of social power.

There is not enough dissent in our media to alter the path of current policies. Any voice that does not agree with the mainstream is derided or ignored. Anyone who actually looks for facts rather than slogans is laughed away. The media has failed.

Look at the Patriot Act. They are a direct threat to the Bill of Rights and our Constitution. If the government labels you a "terrorist," it doesn't matter if there is no evidence. You no longer have rights to an attorney, or a jury trial by your peers.

That piece of paper — the Constitution — holds us together as a nation. Millions of citizens have sworn to preserve that document against all enemies, both foreign and domestic. When a political crisis occurs, the American people react to it in a manner our elite have never anticipated.

Iraq became the new enemy after the Soviet Empire dissolved into fifteen separate countries. The dynastic power elite needed a credible "outside enemy," even if they had to invent one, to maintain social power, to justify the military budget, and to control the Middle East oil, and natural gas, prices.

Iraq was invaded after it was weakened by the First Gulf War and the United Nations inspectors had disarmed Saddam of the most dangerous weaponry. The collaboration of the second Bush regime, and the misleading propaganda of the media, prepped the gullible public to support the Iraq invasion. The terrorists who attacked the World Trade Center were enemies of the secular Iraqi government. The Iraq war did 'fly on the big lie.' The selected resident president has been a successful serial prevaricator thanks to neo-con speechwriters.

The oil people are the wealthiest and most powerful families on the planet — with the exception of international bankers. All industrial societies need oil and natural gas. And it's the oil people who got control of most of the nation's coal and uranium, too.

What were they after in Iraq, if not energy monopoly? Enron was in England, India, Brazil, and Argentina and even bought a wind farm near Palm Springs. The oil barons gave the trust fund baby $35 million to beat John McCain in the primary elections; big companies were not interested in financial election reforms. How else can they support all sides? They conducted a slanderous lying and misleading whisper campaign against one candidate after another.

The proliferation of radio, TV, and corporate printed media, as well as textbooks, has to some extent given us access to far more information, but it has also made us far more vulnerable to persuasion by those who control the message. We no longer hunt for scraps of information and struggle to puzzle together our own interpretation. We are fed messages, or hammered with half-truths and emotion-laden stories, bombarded so much that we can't even clear our minds to think for ourselves.

This has made the populace easy victims to half-truths, deception, a withholding of the facts and the use of outright lies. The CIA would call it dis-information. The secrecy of government agencies hides crimes as well as corruption, thus the perpetrators of malfeasance are not brought to justice.

Saddam was a CIA asset when he was a twenty-five-year-old assassin. He rose to power by 'killing' his way to the top. He was 'our kind of guy,' as long as US business interests had access to Middle Eastern oil. The US government supported him when he warred with Iran. Bush Sr. assured Saddam that we had no interest in his dispute with Kuwait. Then we used Saddam's aggression as an excuse for the initial Gulf War. Bush gave the green light, and then bushwhacked Saddam.

He "bushwhacked" Manuel Noriega, too. The invasion of Panama happened when Manuel tried to blackmail Bush as the CIA was running arms and cocaine; besides, they wanted to keep Panama's canal. Manuel was a CIA asset, too. But he should never have underestimated a former CIA director. Spooks are called spooks for good reason. Secrets and the shredding of documents alleviated his anxiety. Both major political parties were compromised! The cover-up continues.

Kuwait was accused of drilling into Iraqi oil using slant drilling — a practice not unfamiliar to Texas oil crooks. There was a border dispute, and Saddam needed oil revenue and several other issues. The Bush regime wanted an excuse to set up bases in the Middle East in order to control the world's oil supply in order to control oil prices; and for certain other reasons of geopolitics as well. They said they were afraid of fundamentalist revolutions threatening Saudi Arabia; one would have to take into account who organized, funded and trained today's militants.

We had cozy relations with Arabia from World War II onward; it was then that Franklin Roosevelt committed to defend the Royal House of Arabia. The United States replaced the British as political players in the Middle East, as the British and French were losing their colonial empires. Much later, Franklin D. Roosevelt guaranteed the continuation of the Saudi Dynasty.

Kim Roosevelt, and the OSS, had overthrown the democratically elected government of Mosaddegh in Iran because he nationalized Iran's oil resources. No one likes to have their income stream taken away. The oil barons lost control over Iran's oil when the Iranian Revolution surprised the CIA. The Shah who replaced him was America's ally and a buffer with the Soviet Union.

Our dynastic elite still wants to retake Iran, and that means war. John McCain wants war with Russia; Trump knows better than to play that hand because it's clearly unwinnable. Instead, he talks about Iran. Is that winnable? Do you have a son ready to fight it? The business media have to propagandize the population, before each planned war. The right-wing think-tanks, and the Pentagon, spin the "news." They are spinning us today about North Korea and Iran; and the fake news about Russia gets crazier every day. They say that Russia has "moved to NATO's doorstep" when it is NATO that is expanding aggressively into nations that have been Russia's buffers for centuries. They say Russia invaded Ukraine, meaning that when the US made a move on their submarine base in Crimea, Russia caught them at it and shut them out.

The original plan to invade the Middle East occurred when Henry Kissinger was a presidential advisor and the OPEC was first formed. Kissinger, an advisor to Israel as well as to Washington, was a minion of the Banking and Oil Rockefeller dynasty. His protégé was Paul Wolfowitz.

The election of Clinton interrupted the plan to invade the Middle East. It is no accident of history that Bush Sr., Dick Cheney, Bush Jr., and Condi (Chevron) Rice all have backgrounds and interests in the oil business. They are not the problem; it is the people who financed their careers that are the problem.

In true Machiavellian fashion, the real decision makers are insulated from responsibility as they practice indirect rule. They have cut outs and bureaucracies to do their bidding and they would even deny that they have power to maintain the myth that we are a democracy. The dynastic power elite funds the governments we do not deserve.

US intelligence gave the Saudi government a look at satellite photos of Saddam's armies posed on the border of Kuwait. They may have even told them that Saddam was poised on the border of Arabia. That panicked the Saudis into allowing American bases to be established in the Kingdom, which otherwise seem to them a threat and an insult to the holy places of all Islam.

This did not sit well with many Muslims, and if anyone had wanted to call up armies of volunteers to participate in a war on America, it would have been a piece of cake. Islamic peoples do not want new crusaders or new colonialism in their midst. Wahhabism in particular would like to revive the Islamic civilization and unite the nations. The appearance that America had invaded Islamic lands spurred Jihad, or holy wars. The under-educated George W. Bush even mentioned the word "crusade," removing any doubt as to the imagery. That is a dynamite word in the Middle East.

The Islamic world stretches from Morocco to the Philippines. They have already suffered the heavy hand of Western colonialism for hundreds of years. But today, an endless "war on terrorism" guarantees profits for arms manufacturers. The war debt is pure profit for the banking and oil interests, while it bankrupts the country. They plan a war economy while they kill "new deal" programs and distract us from a faltering economy. Wars equal profits, but not for the average person.

Osama bin Laden was a CIA asset, as we funded him in a holy war against the Soviets that had invaded Afghanistan. The CIA supported the anti-Soviet effort in Pakistan and Afghanistan. The Bush Family had ties to the family of the bin Ladens. After 9/11, the bin Ladens were flown out of the US while no American airline was supposedly allowed to fly. The terrorist attack, supposedly not foreseen, panicked the nation, along with anthrax, into give the un-elected resident power to wage pre-emptive wars. The anthrax was weapons grade and suspiciously came out of our own government laboratories.

Our military did not intercept the attackers: they were on stand-down when the hijackers were flying. We had a defense system that did not defend.

Their response, or lack of it, leads observers to the conclusion that this was a massive deception to mobilize the people, making them so fearful, they would give the usurper power and even suspend the Bill of Rights in favor of the Patriot Act.

The outside threat drove the public into the laps of right-wingers who provoked fundamentalism in the Middle East. Aiding a right-wing government in Israel did not help either.

A craven Congress has failed the people. The Patriot Act does not assault Al Qaeda. It curtails our freedom and security. This is George Orwell's warning of a corporate world, where serious lies drown the truth.

Hitler carried out the same type of operation when the Nazis burned down the Reichstag and panicked the people to give him dictatorial power. They blamed communists, killed them, and then moved on to killing social democrats, the blind, the crippled, the retarded, the mentally ill, veterans from World War One, and criminals, before he targeted the Gypsies, the Jews and Slavs. Hitler didn't invent the idea of creating a super race. He was following Gobeneau, Nietzsche, Hegel, Charles Darwin, and especially Herbert Spencer and William Graham Sumner. The Italian fascist invasion of Ethiopia also encouraged Hitler, as American isolationists and conservatives pulled us out of the League of Nations.

There is no exit plan for US troops in Iraq because the neocons plan to stay there, with bases and a puppet government. As of 2017, calls are being made to send more troops back in, not to bring them home. The idea that Russia, and not our "friend" Qatar which hosts US fighter jets, aims to build a pipeline through Syria to the Mediterranean, should not be overlooked. Only the US has a right to do such things!

Our military has 724 bases overseas, and secret bases, so we can kidnap, torture and kill people. (Ghost prisoners leave no paper trail). We have new bases in the heart of Asia — a dream of Captain Mahan in order to control the world. The neo-con regime has cost this country allies that we had for two hundred years. Meeting in Brazil, diplomats met and wore pins that said, "What are we going to do about the United States?" Islamic countries view us as a world threat because we have battle fleets in every ocean. Worldwide wars could be on our horizon. Regional wars are now going on all the time.

The neo-cons lie daily through major propaganda campaigns by the major networks. They have apologists, analysts, and journalists who only care about their own jobs and ignore unpleasant facts and vital information. The whole nation is spinning in confusion and fear. Cigarettes will kill more Americans than religious fanatics. Honest reporters are fired and blackballed if they write about the crimes of Teflon elitists. Some just sell out and join the bandwagon of the gullible headed for additional wars, for the profit of our dynastic elite families.

America is under attack by a right-wing cabals trained and funded by the same dynastic power elite families that formed "The American Liberty League," in 1933. They planned to install a fascist government because they feared an American revolution against their economic empires. This occurred during the depression or failure of unregulated capitalism. Their progeny, accomplished through evolution, what their grandparents failed to achieve, which was the social control of every important institution, including the Supreme Court!

Do you know what a reactionary Herbert Hoover was? He wanted to re-install the Russian Czar in Russia. There may be more than 70 to 100 right-wing organizations with real clout. There were originally 156 American Liberty League families in 1933. Their idea of 'liberty' was to create a totalitarian state wrapped in blind patriotism to the flag. The corporations they control are household names. They own the economy. Now do you understand the significance of the Patriot Act?

Economic power has been translated into political power. The people do not own the media, as even the Public Broadcasting System has pulled in its horns and offers goofy feel-good programs about antiques rather than seeking to counter the Ministry of Propaganda. We have plutocracy even though we teach democracy in the schools. People now realize that we have special interest government and that we are not a republic.

Lobbyism, seniority systems in legislative bodies, purchased candidates, public relations companies, and media corporations were some of the things that enabled the few — the self-proclaimed 'best,' to be above the rest.

Yale did a lot of research with drugs like LSD; not for recreational purposes. Our elite are interested in reducing the population and controlling what's left. Automation and robots are beginning to replace the workforce. There are going to be a lot of unemployed young people around, until a solution is found. Youth are famously easy to enroll in revolutions. Therefore, the social engineers have been studying how to lead people, and lead them astray, using entertainments, distractions, and various methods to 'manage' them. Sort of like the book *Brave New World.* The control of textbooks is also vital when you wish to raise a malleable population. There is a reason why public education is under-funded and vouchers are offered.

Who owns the public relations companies, and who did they target to control your opinions? You have always been the target of manipulation. The propaganda ministries have been all too successful in bamboozling us. The big lies by government and big business have us fighting wars abroad, while we neglect the educational, transportation, health, and environmental needs at home. We got the military industrial complex that President Eisenhower warned us about in his farewell speech to the nation. Neo-cons are killing the social welfare programs every day. The strong do not care for the weak and the weak endure what they must. Neo-cons are social Darwinists in action. The Greeks understood the dangers of unchecked power.

We only have freedom of the press if we own the press, but we do not. The public is bewildered by worldwide protests against US imperial policies. Other societies fear US military power, and they fear us. Yet Americans somehow think our troops should be welcomed as liberators, wherever they go. Even though no one invited them in, and we have a history of attacking functioning nations and leaving them utterly destroyed.

There is not enough dissent in print. Good journalists have been fired, blackballed, and murdered. Writers cannot expose Teflon-coated businesses and criminal families with their massive fortunes. The privileged commit crimes with impunity. Their sponsored candidates can be used and discarded once the public becomes aware of political corruption.

We got the worst government money can buy. It could not have happened without the complicity of privately owned mainstream media. The concentration of information power has led us to the current situation: around six companies control most of what we read, see, and hear.

Just a few decades ago, America had over fifty major news sources, and nobody raised much alarm over the mergers and buy-outs. The CIA has actually got into our media, favoring some reporters for news and even penetrating the media with agents. Notice that the media is circumspect regarding our secret agency that has levels of secrecy that would bewilder their own personnel. When a journalist gets his income from the government, he is no longer an objective news reporter. Some members of the CIA have used journalistic cover to spy on other nations. Read about Frank Wisner and the "Mighty Wurlitzer." The people should have been alarmed when the Pentagon set up its own propaganda bureau.

The American people are not going to have safe days in the future. They do not have enough information to protect themselves from the neo-conservative agenda.

Chapter 6: A Society Built on Lies Eventually Dies

At one time, a society built on lies would eventually, slowly, die. In the nuclear missile age, our death could happen with scientific alacrity. A society that propels itself into the future, on illusions, endangers itself. The United States is not a Super State.

The paper on Sunday morning, like most days, is mostly adverts and sales, and commercial garbage destined for the trashcan — a waste of good trees, and another salvo in the barrage of consumer teasers that aim to get us out shopping. Yesterday, I could not burn a log in the fireplace to keep warm, as the San Joaquin Valley air quality was not clear enough, and using the fireplace would have meant polluting it further. Last summer, on a doctor's advice, I helped move my sister to Whidbey Island where there is fresher air; still, it took months for her valley cough to disappear. The air pollution is damaging the lungs of young children and is thinning out the lungs of the more senior aged people. The first to die of lung diseases were those killed by Hollywood (the stars who promoted smoking), Madison Avenue, and the Southern tobacco companies.

The destruction of the World Trade Center is said to have killed 3,500, or by some reports, 5,000. The tobacco holocaust, perpetrated by the corporate elite, kills 400,000 US citizens annually, and millions more abroad — that is four million lives in a decade.

Sponsored congressional representatives protect the corporations; they shield corporate crime and malfeasance and that is why common people disrespect them.

Public relations companies exist to manipulate the public attitudes toward social institutions owned by the dynastic power elite, which are privately owned propaganda ministries. Lobbyism eroded democracy in America, that little that ever existed.

The myth that we are a democratic society is perpetuated in the newspapers, magazines, movies, and radio stations, and by the talking heads of television. School children are taught that we are a democratic society and can choose our leaders. This is all an illusion fostered by the small group of people who really own and operate our society. Politicians that may have wanted to represent the American people had long been culled out in the primaries. The big money went to the candidates that would not curb corporate power. The privately-owned media ignore any candidate that threatens their control.

The dynastic power elite rule indirectly. They are not visible power players, as were the monarchs and aristocrats of the past. They deny they have power and hide in the shadows of our history when they can.

For some time now, most Americans have realized that TV airtime, and campaign contributions by the super wealthy, have deprived them of representation. Money does not necessarily mean free speech. Social problems like crime, inadequate health care, massive unemployment, and water and air pollution, exist because they are not high priority items in the eyes of the economically privileged.

Another great myth is that the market determines economic decisions. The 'unseen hand' of Adam Smith conveys, in reality, a plutocrat that manages his own vast fortune and corporate bureaucracies, and also numerous so-called public companies and pension funds. Workers and consumers do not make the big decisions. The total society is unbalanced because economic power has been transformed into political power. Most people are without representation or a voice in social affairs.

Insurance companies, drug companies, industrial corporations, banking institutions, and energy companies, all have representation in Congress. You, and the rest of the people, are just the water they swim through.

Now we have Donald Trump. Whatever you may think of him, he was elected. That's more than George W. Bush can say. But before Trump was even inaugurated, there were calls to remove him. If he had any constructive ideas and real intention to try to set things right, we will never know, as he is not being given a chance. Can someone who believes in democracy say "Not my president" to a man who just won an election? Isn't that treason? Would anyone have been allowed to say that about Barack Obama?

When the current business cycle goes bust, Trump will be blamed. But these conditions were set during the Bush and Obama years and things are now too broken to be fixed, especially with the country divided. We have massive amounts of private and public debts. Foreign wars will not solve the business cycle of the privately owned economy.

We have declared ourselves winners in a cold war with communists, and now have two or more 'real' wars going on at any given time. Convinced of our own might and military power, we destabilize sovereign nations from Iran, Libya and Syria to North Korea and many others.

The neo-conservative right-wing government has cost us allies that we have had for over a hundred years. We have undermined the United Nations and this too frightens other societies. Right-wing ideologues will create conflicts that will bleed our youth and diminish our treasury. This is an unacceptable price for the people to pay for the profiteering of our privileged dynastic power elite.

There was a belief that the corporations and their majority owners could get rich again by grabbing the resources of the Middle East; they believed that we could impose puppet governments on Afghanistan and Iraq; they assumed we were world leaders, but — we have few followers. Other societies will continue to resist our economic imperialism. Other nations will not accept our cultural domination of the world via the media, foreign bases, and military threat. We have our battle fleets in every ocean.

When they are better informed, the American people will not support the hidden agenda that is coming out of the Heritage Foundation, CATO, the American Enterprise Institute, the Project for the new American Century, the Federalist Society, the Taxpayers Union, Sound Economy, Ford, Rockefeller, Pew, Sloan, Root, Sams, Avery, E. F. Hutton and whatever conservative or neo-con organization that subverted real democracy. And they will stop falling for the Soros-sponsored destabilization programs that range from sit-ins to street demonstrations to what looks an awful lot like practice for a coup.

The Patriot Act rendered the constitution null and void. Touch voting machines will not correct the fraud in Florida, especially when they are constructed by privately owned companies of the right-wing, or a Republican Senator. Who can trust a government founded on spin, half-truths, lies, disinformation, advertising, and cover-ups?

The entertained, propagandized, disinformed, under informed, and distracted citizen will experience "shock and awe" in the new "World Order." The people will not recover democracy until they kill trust foundations. They gave us a hereditary aristocracy that believed too much in private fortunes, private schools, and private clubs. Companies of limited liability, and now a privately owned government, are a national liability. It takes a long time for the public to become aware of the past success of evolutionary secret politics.

This would not have occurred without a quiescent and complicit media. Decades of indoctrination have had its effect on our citizens. Notice that we are deluged with advertisements to buy, buy and buy. Advertisers will bombard you daily with communications. Notice how they flood the airwaves — even the airwaves are being privatized.

Chapter 7: Mesopotamia, Darfur, and Somalia, Deserve Some Examination...

Mesopotamia has a six thousand year old civilization that has been over-run by Aramaeans, Amorites, Chaldeans, Hittites, Medes and Persians, Hellenes, Parthians, Romans, Turks, Mongols, and the British. Winston Churchill used airplanes and poisonous gas on the "tribes" — as he referred to them — as the Western powers carved up the Ottoman Empire. So the Iraqi people have had previous experience of what a loving, gentle Christian society can do to them. The first Gulf War has been characterized as a "one-sided slaughter." We mowed down Iraqi forces and bombed the country to pieces. Never mind that Saddam had been a CIA asset whom we armed, and backed, in a war with Iran because the Iranians kicked our oil companies out with the Iranian Revolution!

Sanctions against Iraq killed over 800,000 Iraqi people — mostly children — before we bombed and missiled the first electrical grid, the water treatment plant, along with the military installations. One half of the populations of Iraq were under the age of eighteen. They will not forget the "shock and awe" tactics used against them. Every time we break into a house to capture and kill a civilian, a new resistance will be created. We won the military war, but we will lose this war against their civilians.

Why? Because all we are doing is making sure they have good reason to hate us more deeply than anything else. The religious, language and cultural barriers are real; they do not admire us and do not wish to be like us, any more than we wish to be like them. The best we can now hope for is for three divided states; the Kurds separate from the Sunni and Shiites.

If we stay, there will be continual civil war and if we leave there will be civil war. At this stage factions are shooting as well as voting. The fact that we sent death squads into that mess did not help. We won the technological war — we cannot win the political war. We can only delude ourselves, as we do great harm, even bombing individual houses — the use of white phosphorus has killed families. Under the best of circumstances, with our "precision" bombs, we supposedly missed the intended targets 70% of the time.

We lost this war when we 'barbecued' women, old men, babies, and children. We lost this war when we tortured and killed prisoners. The neo-conservatives behind the scenes in Washington have grabbed the "tar baby" of the Middle East. We can prop up a puppet government and try to keep all those bases we are building. This society will pay a heavy price for Iraqi oil, and the natural gas of Central Asia. This war is going to expand, not wind down.

There are other members of the sleeping Islamic civilization that we have now awakened, with a very rude awakening indeed. The United States is involved in other conflicts, in Africa. Our Christian right-wingers, and our government, have given support to the "People's Liberation Army" in the Darfur region of Sudan. Black Christians have rebelled against the Arab Moslem government, resulting in a massive loss of life and the displacement of nomadic tribes. A separate Moslem black rebellion is also at war with the central government using genocide and rape, and ending in broken peace agreements. There are denials that oil and natural gas are factors in that conflict, however in this age of blatant lies natural resources and mineral rights may be the core issues involved in the tragic conflict.

Another conflict is in Somalia, between competing tribal warlords and their clans. The Bush Sr. Administration put lightly-armored American troops in the region, supposedly on a humanitarian mission regarding food and relief supplies to famine victims. What was our national interest in the region? Was it really food aid? Why are we not feeding the starving Syrians trapped in Deir-ez-zor and the Iraqis in Mosul? At least we caused those problems and are responsible for outcome. In Somalia, we are just meddling. Then Bush lost the election and Bill Clinton inherited a problem that led to "Black Hawk Down." We lost two helicopters and our dead were dragged through the streets of Mogadishu. Why?

The troops had intervened in Somali politics in an effort to arrest a warlord after a Pakistani U.N. force was attacked incurring considerable loss of life. Neither Administration told the people that *six oil companies* had signed contracts with a previous leader who was assassinated. Oil companies did not tell the whole story because people might question the policy of using troops to make Somalia safe for investment purposes.

The only newspaper in the United States that mentioned the oil and natural gas factor was the Los Angeles Times. Too often, the privately-owned press aligns itself with power rather than challenge the hidden motives of our elite. Much of our media ignore important stories to protect the status quo.

More bad news: The US is still interfering in Somalia. The spilling of blood does not diminish our thirst for oil and natural gas. Anyway, our weapons and support are one more means of population control. Henry Kissinger thought it a good thing for Iran and Iraq to fight and destroy each other. Our elite wanted both countries to lose so that the oil companies, and natural gas companies, could move back into those rich fields.

Do most Americans realize that there was an arrest warrant issued for the Rockefeller disciple, Henry Kissinger? He is accused of massive war crimes in Latin American and Vietnam, Laos, and Cambodia, and has to avoid traveling to Belgium and many other countries to avoid indictment. That should tarnish the illusion that we are a nation of laws.

Chapter 8: Advice for Our Enemies

The US government has made enemies in Afghanistan and Iraq, in Central and South America, Africa, and in Asia and the Middle East.

When American troops invaded Afghanistan, they allied themselves with some tribes (the so-called "Northern Alliance") that fought the Taliban and Al Qaeda. The American troops traveled with General Dustin. American air power, and Russian armor, defeated the Taliban and Al Qaeda forces. A number close to seven thousand surrendered.

General Dustin told the prisoners they would not be harmed if they surrendered; some TV journalists have it on tape. The General had his troops commandeer trucks, and containers, to transport the prisoners to a distant prison compound. The helpless prisoners were jammed into the metal containers, they were overcrowded and without sufficient water or food. It was hot. Within twenty minutes they were crying for air. The Northern Alliance troops shot holes in the sides of the containers, killing, and wounding their helpless captives.

An Irish filmmaker got the story and managed to reach European audiences including the European Parliament. American media ignored the atrocities committed in the Afghanistan massacre of Taliban in the "Death Convoy". News team interviewed some of the shooters, and another general, who described the Afghan massacre.

When the trucks stopped for gas, an Afghan asked what that horrible smell was. A driver pointed to the containers on the back of the trucks. Blood was leaking from the containers. Days later the trucks arrived at a prison that was run by American soldiers. The containers held dead and dying prisoners. Parched men had licked the sweat off each other, and had even bitten one another to gain precious moisture. The stench of feces, urine, and blood was mixed with rotting flesh. The Americans would not accept the cargo and the trucks were ordered out back into the desert.

An Afghan witness says that Americans were present when prisoners were shot, along with the wounded. The valiant Americans did not render aid nor did they follow the Geneva Conventions; they did not stop the massacre. It was reported that American Advisors told the Northern Alliance soldiers to bury the bodies before satellites came over, as they would film the bodies. When it was discovered that there was a large discrepancy between the number of prisoners originally captured and those left alive, Pashtun-speaking villagers were rounded up and added to the detainees to round up the numbers. More innocents were scooped up to hide these atrocities.

Photographs have revealed that prisoners were tortured and killed while in the care of American troops, and "abused" by intelligence interrogators. Of course, the Pentagon chose to exhibit over-zealous lower ranking non-coms to take the blame and shame. Whom do I hold responsible?

I hold John Foster Dulles and Allen Dulles responsible. Also Robert Murphy, General Beedle Smith, Charlie Thayer, General Draper, and Gustav Hilger. Why? Because they were so concerned with keeping Russia from becoming a rival that they would stop at nothing to develop vicious and in inhuman techniques to wage war. They adopted Nazi practices, took them to a new level, and later trained special forces in Latin America to overthrow governments there. They sent death squads out around the world. We became the enemy. The School of the Americas, at Ft. Benning Georgia, taught torture to US and foreign soldiers. They recently changed the name. (Did we throw people out of helicopters in Vietnam, and poison wells?)

The Dulles Brothers, at one time, worked for the United Fruit Company that historically opposed any democratic social movements in the Caribbean, and Central America. They also worked with American corporations that had ties with Nazi Germany. These brothers were avid anti-communists regarding their foreign policies. The Dulles Brothers aided Guatemala in killing five thousand communists there. With foreign aid, the CIA had some collateral damage over the decades. Over one hundred thousand people died supporting that death squad democracy. (The local elites killed Indians to get their land).

The United States supports a superficial democracy at home while rigging elections, and has stifled democratic rights for others for decades. Now they do it by training foreign citizens in "democratic protest" and encourage them to break local laws intended to maintain public order; they influence other people's elections, then complain about supposed foreign influence here. The Patriot Act, by the way, is designed to eliminate our own Bill of Rights. Why? And why do you and your neighbors think it is acceptable to look after your comfort instead of standing up and asking questions?

The super-rich fear voting and they fear the "masses." They fear elections — now that it costs so much money to get the "right" candidates elected. Neo-conservatives are elitists that believe in 'unfettered' laissez-faire capitalism. They do not want government regulations that moderate their greed. They only want government when they are able to control it through their minions. They talk of democracy, but they believe that private property interests are supreme, even above public interests.

In Afghanistan, the United States had 'ghost' prisoners that they hid from Red Cross workers. They isolated them and did no paper work on them, and hid them from inspectors. Why? So those prisoners could be tortured or killed without a paper trail. Why are prisoners held off our coast so they cannot enjoy the protection of our laws? They are held there so they can be tried by military tribunals and executed.

There is no other society today that has been so thoroughly misinformed, under informed, mislead and bamboozled. How did it happen? The dynastic power elite used lobbyists, seniority rules in Congress, political advertising, and outright propaganda involving big lies. They created public relations companies and got control over all the major media to spin half-truths and distractions — like Martha Stewart serving time while Hillary Clinton walks away free. They operate all major media, so it was easy to manipulate the people. Journalists and editors, who would print truths, are fired (San Jose Mercury, for example). They must protect their own families.

The Pew family is constantly carrying out polls to find out your opinion (they want to know if you have caught on yet as to how the systems really work). They take the social pulse to make sure you are not ready to revolt, yet. The neo-cons are ready for you, if you do revolt; they have militarized the police. The State National Guards are now under closer control of the Pentagon to contain civil unrest. Ollie North, and the Pentagon, built camps to handle future dissidents. This Republic is already lost.

We are not going to have nice days in the future. Our debts will increase. The government borrowed funds from private banks to fight these current wars. Has it occurred to you that we may become debt slaves to the private banks? Even our children and grandchildren are now in debt! President Jefferson thought that private banks could become a greater threat to our liberties than "standing armies".

Do sheeple really believe that you can spread democracy to other countries by invading them? Those illusions have killed American the Beautiful. Like good Germans, we can deny what our nation is doing, and pretend that we really did not know about the torture and murders. Bad things happen to people who do bad things...

My final advice to enemy troops is this: Do not surrender. You are going to be tortured and/or killed anyway. You are not facing a traditional (much less legendary, or mythical) American Army. The CIA has even killed members of our own government and our own agents, including Green Berets, CID Agents, DEA agents, Army colonels, the families of FBI agents, and General Joseph Stillwell Jr. — three hours before he was to testify to a Congressional Investigation Committee.

Neo-cons like Pearle, Bremer, Wolfowitz, Armitage, and Rumsfeld, etc., do not recognize that you have human rights.

Julian Assange, Private Manning, and Edward Snowden, do not have wild imaginations. They have facts about recent administrations. That is why they face arrest and persecution. Whistle-blowers need protection rather than persecution. They are witnesses to our history.

CHAPTER 9: WHO TAUGHT AMERICANS HOW TO TORTURE? WHEN?

"Lawmakers Stunned by Ghost-Detainee Figure"
— the 'Modesto Bee' newspaper).

"Washington - A senior US Army General, who investigated the abusive treatment of prisoners in Iraq, said yesterday that the CIA may have avoided registering up to one hundred detainees in the US military facilities; a number far higher than the eight cases that Army officials had previously cited." In Senate hearings, senators have been unsuccessful in obtaining documents from the CIA regarding the ghost prisoners. (Secrets hide crimes. The insider joke is, "Criminals In Action.")

This back page article needs elaboration to understand what has happened in our intelligence agencies since the end of World War II.

Ghost prisoners are those that have not been registered with the Red Cross and whose treatment is not in accordance with Geneva Convention rules — rules that the United States agreed on by treaty.

These are prisoners without a paper trail, because they are tortured for information and killed. They become ghosts. The media has gone along with such terms as "hard interrogation" and "prisoner abuse," in order to shelter the public from the truth. However, newspaper accounts have mentioned the deaths of prisoners in Afghanistan and Iraq (latterly, over one hundred). A "contract torturer" was charged in Kabul. That story reached the press, as well as the story of our turning over prisoners to countries in the Middle East that carry out torture, but this is an under-reported story.

We have an atavistic shadow government that has returned us to the Dark Ages. We signed the Geneva Convention to provide protection for *our own* prisoners of war. Since we broke that treaty, our troops are now endangered if captured by Geneva signatories.

The Bush dynasty and other powerful families had financial interests in the United Fruit Company. The Dulles Brothers were attorneys for them at one time. The attorneys negotiated reduced reparations for Germany based on the damages of World War I. Other financial interests included equipment for the Baku Oil fields in Stalin's era; the Manganese mines in the Caucasus Mountains; mines in Poland; Remington Arms; Thompson sub machine guns; railroad couplings; the iron company in Ohio, which made artillery shells in World War II, Prudential Insurance, CBS radio, and the Union Bank of New York (partners of Harriman Brothers), Brown Brothers, Fritz Thyssen, industrialist from Germany had account. The Union Bank of New York funded the destitute Austrian artist Adolf Hitler who was working as a government spy and contacted by the Thule Society. Partners were all Skull and Bonesmen out of Yale and were supporters of the eugenics movement in the US. Other Bush family members had investment in Savings and Loans, CIA drug running, and other scams and cover-ups.

Two months into the Reagan administration, Neil Bush had to cancel a dinner engagement with the Hinckley Family. A Hinckley family member put an explosive bullet two inches from the heart of Ronald Reagan. On television, a shocked John Chancellor managed to mention this information on the air before the Bush public relations minions, and the national media, shut that story down.

Did Marvin Bush and his company Securacom "work" in the World Trade Center for three nights prior to the terrorist attack? Were the custodial and security staff given three nights off, so that work — under the guise of maintenance — could be done on the Twin Towers? One might wonder on what kind of "work" they were doing. People who worked there noted that the security "sniffer" dogs were absent that week. Why do so many New York firefighters, staff, and survivors, relate that they heard a series of bombs going off? Why do so many New Yorkers believe that this was an inside job to manipulate the society and mobilize them for war? It is a fact that it is not possible for airplane fuel, which burns like kerosene, to cause a steel beam to melt. Is the media as complicit as the 9/11 Commissions?

It is amazing that citizens who saw the planes flying into the Towers did not question the photographers who were stationed there to take the pictures as it happened. Some who were detained by police showed up with diplomatic passports. A group of Mossad agents filmed the attack from the flatbed of a truck.

When US intelligence and military adopted the activity of torture, they transformed a society that thought it stood for some ideals into a model of the Dark Ages. Their atavism undermined the Bill of Rights of our Constitution. Government lawlessness undermined our legitimacy.

The majority of American citizens hold liberal values and concerns. They want health, education, welfare for those who truly need it, safe jobs, decent housing, clean air, and safe water for everyone. But, they are saddled with massive spending for arms. Our political institutions are not responding to those needs. Most citizens are very disenchanted with "business as usual."

CHAPTER 10: A SOCIAL COMMENTARY ON AMERICAN SOCIETY

The poor battered American citizen is bombarded by an average of five thousand advertisements a day. Radio, TV, newspaper advertisements, posters, billboards, intrusive telephone calls, and even door-to-door sales people, target each of us.

The dynastic power elite families who own and control the major corporations also have control over most of the media and use it to manipulate the news, and thereby manipulate the public. The controlling of information is a practiced form of social control. Information that is vital to understand what has been happening in America is withheld, or ignored. Limited information is doled out, or hung out, and dis-information can be provided to bring people to false conclusions regarding what has happened, and what may be occurring at any given time.

The people have surely under estimated the cleverness of some of this propaganda. They fall victim to partial truths, slanted or spun information and outright fabrications. Big lies work to deceive the unwary. We are deluged with bad news broadcasts, which show us the reality of murder, mayhem, and disasters. Even though they are real, they are put forth to frighten us and to encourage us to buy guns and to obey orders from the "authorities" without a thought.

Such broadcasts give a lot of airtime to those who do crime. A police state has been set up to "protect us." Look at the Patriot

Act — it sets aside our freedom and liberty. We have been carefully programmed by some media to look for security in purchasing weapons, and to that end, most houses now have guns in them. This fear-driven society now maintains the largest military arsenal in the history of the world. We have a bloated military budget that outstrips a dozen other countries. What has driven us to become so militant and weapon-ized?

We fear terrorists even as our own tobacco companies kill four hundred thousand of us every year! All for the profiteering of you-know-whom. Which is the greater threat?

The idea of social property, or political domination by a monopoly of power, energized the capitalist nations. They sent troops into Russia, trying to restore the Czar and maintain private property rights. At the time, Russia was devastated by a war with Germany that it was losing. Hunger stalked the land. The Russian Revolution was a painful disaster for its people incurring a massive loss of life in a civil war, with outside nations intervening with money, munitions, and foreign troops. The Reds won and consolidated their power by crushing all opposition. It was a naked power struggle.

Anti-communism, and anti-socialism, has been the cornerstone of US foreign and domestic policies since then. We have been programmed to fear and hate the Reds. When the Soviet Empire fell apart into fourteen separate countries, it was no longer a threat. A new enemy had to be created to justify the creation of the warfare state we now have. Iraq, and others, were promoted to fill that void to justify militarism and the massive defense budget — that is now an offense budget — as we attack other nations. Iraq became the outside enemy to provide social cohesion for the established power structure. You must know by now who owns the military industrial complex that President Eisenhower warned us about, in his farewell address to the Nation. The neo- conservatives are dismantling the welfare state every day. We now have a warfare state, and our young men and women are to be sacrificed for massive profits as we go into debt to support the usual suspects. When the Cold War supposedly ended, there was no peace benefit. We made war on Grenada, Panama, Gulf Wars I and II, and Afghanistan. All were supported by a privately owned information system. The neo-conservative social movement is aggressive and hostile. Notice how it targets poor nations with subversion and bribes, or resorts to violence and interventions.

Take a look at our little known history. This is a look at the past in order to understand the phenomenon known as the neo-conservatives; they are not traditional conservatives in the least. Here is their past:

How about baby Bush's call to the President of Argentina re: ENRON. "My daddy is President of the United States, and five American companies will pull out of your country — and collapse your economy — if you do not sell your natural gas at 40% below world prices to ENRON" (according to Mother Jones magazine article).

Dewey Clarridge, Oliver North, and "Jeb" Bush — "Jeb" warehoused illegal cocaine. CIA Director William Casey did not like to kill police officers "unless it was absolutely necessary," e.g., to cover up crimes. Iran/Contra was just a portion of malfeasance. Skull and Bonesmen were on the oversight committee. Senators Kerry and Boren probably held key positions for damage control, using national secrecy as cover.

Neil Bush reportedly received over a billion dollars, bringing down the Savings and Loans. Taxpayers footed the bill when Congress bailed them out. Neil Bush had to cancel his dinner engagement with the Hinckley family. Within several months of the election, a Hinckley boy put an explosive bullet in Ronald Reagan's chest close to his heart. Only a shocked John Chancellor mentioned it before the national media clamped shut. This society has millions of "Good Germans" in it who did not know what was going on.

The record will show that Allen Dulles was right, "Americans do not read books." Not enough of them, anyway — with the exception of yourself. A news reporter had asked Dulles about the Warren Commission Report and the "Magic Bullet." The Warren Commission Report did not mention that Prescott Bush lost $53 million when Fidel Castro nationalized West Indies Sugar. Nor George Bush Sr.'s whereabouts.

A Texas newspaper editor quit counting, after over fifty witnesses to the Kennedy operation were demised with "accidents," "natural causes," and "suicides." Dorothy Killgallen, the only reporter to talk to Oswald alone, died of a heart attack before she could relate what she had learned. The Agency can kill you with a cup of coffee. 'Vinegar Joe' Stillwell's son died of a heart attack three hours before he was to make a deposition before a Congressional hearing regarding Iran/Contra. The CIA did a "limited hangout." The secret hearings and perjury hid the crimes and there was no impeachment.

The crooked system kept operating. There was no reform. This was far bigger than the name applied to it.

Tens of thousands of personnel are doing their jobs not knowing what a cabal has done to undermine the Republic. There are real patriots in the Pentagon and the CIA, and they were the first whistle-blowers that tried to warn the nation about "Shadow Government" and an agency that defied presidents and our laws.

President Harry Truman had the courage to fire Skull and Bonesman Henry L. Stimson. Stimson had violated a written order of the President. Stimson was shocked when that little man from Missouri sent him to clean out his desk. Henry Louis Stimson was escorted out of office in a single day. It is doubtful that a modern day president has that kind of insight and courage, or the ability to do it and stay alive.

You may not know enough to protect our Constitution, nor even save the lives of your young. Think about this: Why did the neo-conservatives create the Patriot Act? You may not know how much the elite fear you and your fellow Americans. They tie us in a web of lies to hide their crimes. National secrecy in our government hides scams, frauds, psychological warfare, murder and the violation of national and international laws. This government is not transparent. It has opaque portions that hide crimes against our citizens and other nations. National secrets not only hide national mistakes but they also hide national crimes. Look at all the enemies we are acquiring? Our progeny will have to pay dearly for the crimes of our current neo-conservative minions. On top of that, our children and grandchildren will inherit massive public debt, payable to private banks. Their "Brave New World" — with Orwellian overtones — will shackle them, as no other generation in our history.

How many citizens know that Henry Kissinger had to flee Belgium to avoid arrest as a war criminal? Remember the secret war in Laos and Cambodia? Carpet-bombing villages? The Hague World Court has a judgment against the United States for crimes committed by Bush Sr." and Ronald Reagan, for the crime by Dewey Clarridge who mined a harbor in Nicaragua. There is a worldwide protest against our invasions and occupations that violate the treaty of Westphalia and ignore international law. It is not popular for us to bribe governments and overthrow those we cannot control.

The privately owned media is not the guardian of democracy or the protector of the former Republic. Your civil rights are being eroded daily. Over one hundred journalists and cameramen have been killed in Iraq and Afghanistan, and you are probably oblivious to the fact. If you think embedded journalists tell us the truth, you are gullible. They do not get the opportunity to carry out independent investigations; they are victims of Pentagon handouts; they are surrounded by people with guns; and they are not only in danger of losing their careers and good names, they are being killed for what they may know. Facts, and the truth, were the very first victims of the Middle East and Central Asian war.

You may not know why anthrax was developed as a military weapon, or why we would revive smallpox for "population control." Americans will not be able to handle the truth of what has happened to our society. You do know that the American Army gave smallpox blankets to American Indians during the Indian wars? The American economy got off the ground with the invasion and stealing of the land for private property interests. Property is sold, traded, or inherited, after peace is established. All great nations are founded on great crimes.

World scientists brought smallpox under control, and now the Pentagon and the CIA have developed biological weapons. Biological weapons are not good military weapons. If "precision" bombs mostly miss, how can we pretend we will be able to control the spread of diseases we unleash?

We are at war with distant cultures that we do not understand. Our government lies to, and steals from, whole countries — and murders their people — and Christian right-wingers, who never saw a conflict with the Ten Commandments, avidly support it. The faithful are sheeple and are highly gullible to patriotic propaganda. Their faith endangers our civilization. We lost friends and allies we had had for two hundred years. The gullible easily accept the apologist, and right-wing, verbal attacks on a candidate's character. Unfortunately, repeated lies are effective in persuading people to accept candidates and aggressive foreign policies that lead to wars.

Our Defense Department became an Offensive Department. Our neo-cons conduct their political behavior as if they are at war, through alternative party programs and with science and facts. They are ideologists saturated with social Darwinism, and they are undermining laws to win and maintain their power. Their political success has emboldened them to embark on new outrages. How did they manage to obtain power? They did this with their great fortunes and access to information. In the last decade, we had access to less foreign news, but received more entertainment and distractions. Reliable media sources were diminished by merges. Around six corporations have replaced over fifty family news sources that we had in the past. We ended up with monopoly news.

Why is it that the Farish family and Warburg family names appear in these different books? Paul Warburg helped create the Federal Reserve Board. The banks — which are private companies, not public utilities — control the interest rates that indebted citizens pay on all loans.

The Fed prints the money, and rents it to the government, putting the government in debt to private financial interests. Shouldn't the government print its own bonds and currency, rather than put itself in debt to the super-rich? The Federal Reserve Act was reportedly passed with some hanky panky involving a Christmas vacation of Congress. The private banks met secretly, off the coast, to plan their strategy. Maybe an elected government should control our money supply and interest rates.

That notion might have been the real reason why Abraham Lincoln and John F. Kennedy were assassinated. Lincoln had the government print "Green backs" to fund the war with the South. Confederate Secretary of the Treasury, Judah Benjamin, stole the entire treasury of the Confederacy and shipped it to a Rothschild bank in London — when General Lee surrendered at Appomattox. President John F. Kennedy proposed to fund social programs with government bonds. It may have been a fatal idea. The folks too big to fail, or jail, would not appreciate such notions.

CHAPTER 11: RETAIL AND WHOLESALE KILLING

An American serial killer was asked why women and children were the victims? He said, "They are easy to kill."

That may be true, and more unarmed civilians are usually probably killed in wars than combatants. Those that are not murdered outright die from starvation, disease, neglect, and so forth; all indirect results of war. War is mass murder. Many people would not accept that definition for human carnage. In the past, wars have been promoted by evoking noble rationales based on race, religion, politics, and economic differences. There are many reasons for humans killing humans on a retail and wholesale basis. This will be discussed further without regard to a timeline. Some history books make war sound glorious and romantic; it is highly doubtful that veterans share that perspective. Especially if they have seen their friends killed, or have suffered themselves in armed combat. Armies and wars have been with us from the beginning of civilization. Standing Armies had their inception when nomadic people collided with stationary farming societies, usually near a river or lake.

This chapter takes a historical view of killers, examining their multifarious motivations. It will cite ancient and recent examples of murder. For example, a local businessman had hired two men to kill his business partner. The criminals gained access to the victim's house, but unfortunately the victim's wife was in the house at the time, and she became a victim of "collateral damage" (a Pentagon term). They were wired, gagged, and stabbed to death. During the incident, the witness was killed to ensure the safety of the guilty. The killers were caught and implicated the instigator of this crime. News accounts attributed economic motivation for the conspiracy, namely greed; a sole owner would not have to share the business profits with an eliminated partner. Crimes rely on secrecy. There may have been ancillary reasons for the murder, as many events have multiple causes. This is an example of a person exacting ultimate power over the existence of another's life.

The first killer I ever interviewed was a boy who always looked quite serious. He was from Los Angeles. A jacket gang had beaten him; his assailants wore dark jackets with a white emblem on the back. Sometime later, he went to a bus stop where a small group of commuters was standing. A young man who was standing in the group, waiting for a bus, was wearing a jacket with the same emblem on the back. The former victim stepped up behind the new victim. He said, "All I saw was red." The abused boy became a killer when he attacked the young man with a switchblade knife. He did not care about the witnesses standing nearby. He did not know the victim personally. It turned out that the victim had not participated in his own assault. Just wearing the uniform of a jacket gang was enough to invite deadly retaliation for a teenage beating.

Misdirected anger has killed many innocent people, those not directly involved in a conflict.

The second young male killer I talked to almost killed another young man with an oak chair in a dayroom. A company of delinquents was sitting smoking, waiting for the lunch hour and a trip to the cafeteria. The potential victim was sitting, looking away toward another Group Supervisor and me. We had a young man in the California Youth Authority who had been born with syphilis. He had stabbed another young man to death at Kezar Stadium in San Francisco, during a sporting event. His file indicated that he was unstable and suffered from general paresis; he was not expected to live very much past adulthood. There had been some name calling earlier in the day that no one had paid much attention to. This killer boy got out of his chair and lifted the chair over his head. It was heavy enough to crack a skull. I yelled loud enough to bring dead silence to the hall. I screamed the young man's name and said, "Put that chair down." There was nothing else I could do from the distance that separated us. My commanding voice froze the potential assailant, and his victim turned and dived for safety under the table. The attacker was known for being impulsive, easily offended, and he lacked control over his emotions. Who knew what damage the spirochetes bacteria were doing to his brain?

I talked to a seventeen-year-old young man, a Chicano boy from Los Angeles. He was committed to the California Youth Authority for murdering a man at a dance. He was a handsome, athletic boy that could have been a movie star. I asked him why he had killed. He said that he was dancing with a girl, and another man cut in on him. The intruder was older and bigger than he was and he felt humiliated by what had happened, so he went home and got his father's .45 caliber pistol and returned to the dance. He killed the intruding man on the dance floor. From the way he talked, I got the impression that this code of conduct was acceptable to him and was a matter of honor and/or of saving face. His anger was entirely justifiable in the context of his experience; in some sub cultures, resorting to violence is axiomatic.

Over time, I learned that many killers had been abused and neglected as children. Though not all abused children develop into killers. Without love, or care, the tortured child may become psychopathic, and a killer. They can be recognized by their habit of carrying weapons; they do not trust others, and their repressed anger can explode at any given time; and their accumulated hate can become misdirected. Seeing 'red' describes the condition of unleashed destructive emotion. In the era of their abuse, children are unable to destroy their parents, or care givers, so their repressed anger is later misdirected at others who may trigger a violent reaction.

However, a survey of those on death row, at Sing Sing Prison, Ossining, New York, indicated that every murderer there had been raised through the types of harsh discipline that could be identified as torture. A woman named Alice Miller discovered the genesis of violence in her book, "For Their Own Good." Today she remains unrecognized for her discovery of what turns individuals into killers. Her work in understanding the toxic curriculum was as important as the discovery, by Louis Pasteur, that germs cause disease. Of course, not all tortured children become homicidal. Why? Because some grow up identifying with figures in their lives that were not pain givers. Many severely abused children grow up modeling their own lives on healthy humane figures, such as a decent parent, relative, or friend. It is possible for them to survive horrendous upbringings by identifying with ministers, teachers, and coaches. Successful people, and all of the above, may become healthy role models for such children if they are able to accept a nonviolent code of conduct to base their lives upon. These abuse survivors seem to be able to reject emulation of their past abusers.

In Europe, nobles carried daggers and swords on their persons so that they might address any insult or slight with an edged weapon. In the Dark Ages, men and women carried knives to cut their food, or in order to 'cut' any threat made towards them. Alexander Hamilton, and Andrew Jackson, resorted to heavy caliber Derringers to settle their affairs of "honor" in dueling codes. There are societies that approve of some killings and will always try to justify their wars, over territory, water rights, and the possession of natural resources.

The Eskimo or Inuit alone did not have national wars, as they had no nation. They had to cooperate in order to survive a harsh environment; they shared their goods and their space, as there was a great deal of it in the Arctic Circle. They even shared their wives with strangers and guests. Of course, this cultural act would violate moral codes in some societies, but it made sense in small villages to expand the gene pool, and avoid inbreeding. In other societies, men would kill in order to have sole access to their women. The environment can shape customs and social behavior.

Historically, nomadic armies swept across Eurasia attacking settlements and cities. Their Siberian ponies gave them mobility to attack across frozen rivers and lakes, thus they attacked Russia in winter. The Mongols destroyed whole cities, if they were resisted. If the population surrendered and gave tribute, they

were spared total destruction. Originally they slaughtered farmers, but when they returned later, there was not enough food
to feed the predatory armies. So the Khan revised his policies
and spared peasants so that his livestock and horde might eat by
stealing the food of the victims.

In some societies war was controlled. In New Guinea, for example, some tribes would stop their warmongering after a few
people were killed, or wounded, and then go home; they did not
decimate the whole tribe. They would be satisfied in the killing
of, or eating of, the stray child or adult that came into their territory. Most smug under-educated Europeans, and Americans, do
not know to this day that some of their ancestors in Europe not
only practiced head hunting but actually consumed their prey.
Anthropologists have found evidence of cannibalism in Switzer-
land, Denmark and other places. Roman historians recorded the
eating habits of the Picts, when they invaded what is now Scotland. The Roman soldiers were disconcerted by the noon lunch
break of the blue clay clad Picts. Wounded and dead Romans
were dragged off to be eaten. No wonder Hadrian wanted a wall
between Pict-land and their colony in Britain.

Regarding Europe — the seat of our inherited civilization —
would it not it be nice if we were all civil to other humans? Too
bad religion, race, and class can be divisive elements in society,
although of course religion does unify groups, as well as cause
conflict between people.

The Celts were known to tie people to trees and burn them,
sacrificing them to animistic gods. In Germany, a well was found
filled with the skulls of young men and women; they were sacrificed at a young age, probably as a religious offering to the
natural gods and goddesses that seemed to have an appetite for
human life. Bogs have revealed the preserved remains of people
and their gold jewelry; their tools and weapons sent to them in
a believed-in after life.

Not all were volunteers. Many societies sacrificed prisoners
of war like the Aztecs. They, like the Egyptians, worshipped the
Sun. They knew that life could not survive without that near
star. The Chinese sacrificed their wives, soldiers, and servants
to serve dead masters when burying emperors or warlords. It
took three hundred years for the sacrifice of Jesus on the cross

to spread through Europe. That sublimation ended the atavistic practices of our ancestors. When humans saw themselves as being all children in the likeness of a god, some protection was offered to the value of human life. Christianity did affect laws, customs and social behavior.

Even with religion and moral codes, killing, and torture did not stop. When religion dominated European life, wars that may have been over territory and resources were of course promoted in terms of differences between the Catholic, Orthodox and Protestant sects. The Crusades sent warring knights and adventurers across Europe and into the Holy Land to battle the rival religion of the Saracens. Conflict with Islam is again visible today. Fundamentalists, theirs and ours, practice killing even though the religions involved proscribe it. People are capable of compartmentalizing their beliefs and this enables them to lie, steal, and kill regardless of their religious training or secular moral codes.

Social thought has historical consequences. 'Thinkers' have had a devastating impact on human history. The social thought content of German philosophers, Hegel and Friedrich Nietzsche, and also of Gobeneau, Charles Darwin, Herbert Spencer, and William Graham Sumner led others to eugenics and murder. Their social thought led to Social Darwinism, Eugenics and the Holocaust. Eugenics came to Yale, and our industrial elite, in 1908. The following are the families that supported the eugenic movement in the United States: Davenport, John D. Rockefeller, George Herbert Walker, the Harriman Brothers, the Brown Brothers, Prescott Bush, the Warburg family, William Farish III, Andrew Carnegie, William Draper, Boyden Gray, and Bowman Gray. The eugenics campaign in the United States was farther reaching than you may realize. Do you know the real reason you were given an I.Q., or achievement, test in school? Do you know anything about the forced sterilization projects in the thirties and forties? Guess why mixed marriages were outlawed....

These may seem to be digressions but the social history is related. The families that supported Eugenics, the "American Liberty League," the Nazi Party in Germany, the "Bund" Nazi Party in America, the "Silver Shirts," the "Crusaders," "America First," and "Social Justice," overlapped.

Some of the same families founded, and funded, the Heritage Foundation, the American Enterprise Institute, CATO, Sound Economy, Olin, Ford, Rockefeller, the Hoover Institute, Coors, Pew, Colgate, E.F. Hutton, Raskob, Sloan, the Federalist Society, the Hitler Project, and maybe a hundred other right-wing foundations and organizations. They accomplished, with evolution, what their grandparents and parents failed to do in 1933 — to displace democracy with a privately owned corporate state. They were against big government until they penetrated the House, the Senate White House, and the Supreme Court with neo-conservatives. Now they wrap themselves in the flag and scare the world with invasions and subversions. We lost allies we had for over two hundred years!

Hegel taught that thesis, versus anti-thesis, results in a synthesis. Some people recognized that opposing social movements brought about either conflict, or synthesis. Some dynastic families learned this principle. For example, the Rothschild banking family funded the Russian Czar in his campaign to fight against England in the Crimean War. The dynastic Rothschild family also bought up all the gambling debts of the King of England and his wagering brother. After penetrating the Bank of England, they loaned money to England, thereby financing the Crimean War from the other side. By backing opposing sides they were ensured profits from the war. In fact, when you support both thesis and antithesis, hedging your bets means the third party can never lose and can control eventual outcomes.

The Dynasty of Samuel Bush used Hegelianism. This American industrialist provided Remington Arms and Thompson Arms to the Kaiser of Germany in World War I. Samuel Bush was also on the War Production Board of the United States. He provided Arms for the American Army that fought Germany! He profited from both sides of the conflict. He could not lose, no matter who won or lost the war. In the 1930s, Senator Nye verbally attacked the Bush dynasty in the Senate for being one of the "Merchants of Death." The Bush family made artillery shells for the Army during World War II, and in so doing accumulated massive profits.

Regarding another industrial family: The du Pont family came over here around the time of the 1812 War. They made gunpowder and munitions for all our subsequent conflicts. They backed the "American Liberty League Plot of 1933." One hundred and fifty six of our most powerful industrial families feared a potential revolution by farmers and workers. The Russian Revolution, by workers and peasants, frightened our dynastic power elite families. After the Stock Market crash of 1929, the US nation really suffered. Political movements on the right and left formed to find answers to the crisis of a failed economy that engendered massive business failures, closed factories, made banks bankrupt, and created sudden poverty and mass unemployment.

Our elite planned to kill Franklin Delano Roosevelt, and Cordell Hull, and supplant democracy with a fascist state; the plot failed because the Military would not go along with it. General Douglas McArthur, and Lt. Colonel Dwight D. Eisenhower, drove the veterans — the Bonus Army marchers — out of Washington. The military exceeded orders and burned down a "Hoover Ville" (a shantytown). This occurred before the inauguration of President Franklin D. Roosevelt. Remember, the plot occurred after the attempt on Roosevelt's life had failed when a woman spectator pushed the arm of the "lone crazed gunman" and the Mayor of Chicago was shot instead, and later died of his injuries. (That liberal thereafter won four elections and served almost sixteen years. The neo- conservatives today have great fear of liberals. That is why they are slandered in the privately owned media. Liberals threaten the power interests of the neo-conservatives).

The Army used tanks, tear gas, and bayonets to prevent the planned putsch by the far right. (the Industrialists) The Wall Street lawyers had been to France to study the Grand Feux movement, the Italian Fascist Party, and Adolf Hitler's Brown Shirts. Congress covered up the plot and did not call any plotters to testify. They had clients rather than constituents, even then like today. The Philadelphia Record, and Paul Comly French, was the only media to reveal the true facts to the unaware populace.

The British and American elite families feared social property rights and solely supported private property rights. This was natural because they were the wealthiest citizens who owned most of the nation's wealth. The richest feared the democratic, vote, and the mass of people. They still fear you. That is why they always want to control your thought and behavior. Public relations and media companies have represented the owners of those companies. Public opinion is important and that is why we are deluged with propaganda, and it is also why vital information is left out of some history books.

Remington rifles and Olin bullets were the weapons to be provided for the American Putsch. Thomson sub-machine guns were given to Nazi thugs for their street battles with Communists. Is that not an interesting piece of history! Guess which dynastic family was involved in that sale of Arms. Actually, George Herbert Walker, the Harriman Brothers, Prescott Bush, and the Brown Brothers were all Skull and Bonesmen from Yale. They, and the British elite, funded Adolf Hitler and the Brown Shirts from 1923 until 1942. Why? Probably because their Union Bank of New York was an investment bank, which had funds belonging to Fritz Thyssen — the industrialist who funded Adolf Hitler. Our government seized the bank in 1942, during the war.

The Eugenics movement was popular in England, thanks to Charles Darwin — the British philosopher Herbert Spencer, Major Leonard Darwin (Charles Darwin's son), and even Winston Churchill. Churchill always supported the British Empire and the domination of other races by Anglo Saxons. Churchill even believed that there was such a thing as the English race. He overlooked the fact that the people of Great Britain included ancestral tribes of Northumbrians, Iberians, Celts, Romans, and Scandinavians. Churchill ended up as Britain's Prime Minister in order to wage war against Germany.

The European empires were established through invasion and war, and the subsequent taking of natural resources from weaker societies. Racism was a part of the aggression that the elite supported. They also supported social Darwinism, the survival of the fittest, and the elimination of the weak.

In order to understand what has happened in the United States today, it is necessary to return to historical facts. President Truman created the centralized agency to prevent the future recurrence of the events of Pearl Harbor. That agency completely failed to prevent the attack on the World Trade Center buildings.

General Donovan thought the OSS was ideal for running "Black Operations." Those operations often violated International and National laws. They assassinate (wet operations), overthrow other governments, engage in the blackmailing of individuals in Congress, execute scams, bribe foreign leaders, and kill any of their own, and other agents of the government, that would reveal their crimes. The OSS evolved into the CIA. The CIA failed to see the Iranian Revolution coming and the dissolution of the Soviet Union into fifteen separate countries.

The populace was warned by members of the agency that a shadow government was being created, but the warning was unheeded by Congress. We have had a spate of suspicious air crashes — eliminating Congressmen who opposed certain interests, and future candidates like John Kennedy Jr., and foreign figures who were inconvenient. Like the 'accidental' crash of the 'puppet' who ran Panama, before Manuel Noriega became an arms and drug running partner of CIA. The national leader of Pakistan also died in an air crash before the current General became our 'boy' chasing Osama bin Laden. Ron Brown died in an air crash in the Balkans. When an autopsy was performed on him there was no plausible explanation for the hole on the top of his head.

Lt. Commander Al Martin, a Naval Intelligence Officer who worked with the CIA for fourteen years, revealed those crimes. Dewey Clarridge was involved in the mining of a harbor in Nicaragua that was a violation of International law. Because of the media censorship, few citizens know that "the Hague War Tribunal" has a judgment against the United States for that crime. Reportedly, Dewy also blew up some investigative journalists in Central America.

The concluding example is this: Populist presidential candidates were culled out in the primary elections. The du Pont family members supported Gore and Lieberman in an earlier presidential selection. Their spawn ran the foundations that provided neo-conservatives for the current Bush-Cheney regime. Again we see the Hegelian principle applied to maintain political power. The dynastic power elite families hedged their bets to get their favored candidates in office; they practiced indirect rule; they have successfully hidden their social power. Their economic power, amounting to billions of dollars, has been translated into political power. This dis-enfranchised the majority of citizens who are not represented in Congress.

The neo-cons gained social control with public relations companies, ownership of major media companies, and lobbyism. The goal of Skull and Bones has been the control of society for the past two hundred years. The TV programs program the viewers. Social control is their aim and they want to suppress dissent in Congress, and in this society. Neo-conservatives are not traditional Republicans as both major political parties have been penetrated.

The people who rule America today fear democracy and they fear your freedom. They are afraid of your numbers, and they have a fear of fair elections. Who do you think made some of those black box voting machines? In the Bush years, Karl Rave's boast of 300 years of rule was based on an insider's knowledge and that is why we experienced two fraudulent selections. Ohio, Texas, Nevada, and Florida, experienced voting irregularities, again. The American people never had a chance to choose a President for peace. After all, both George Bush Jr., and John Kerry, were members of the "Brotherhood of Death," the Order of Skull and Bones. Neither candidate proposed bringing our men and women home to safety. There will be no peace. The Welfare State has been replaced by the Warfare State and most citizens, like editors and publishers, are oblivious and under-informed.

The Secret Order wants the destruction of our society to be so bad that we will gladly accept a New World Order government, a government of all the people and its resources — all privately owned. The neo-conservatives have plans for everyone. Some even believe that corporations will replace the nation states. We will all be feudal slaves of one corporation or another, with no liberty, no self-determination, and no option.

They own the corporations, they support unregulated capitalism, and they are against government — unless they control it. When in control, they promote patriotism and wear little flags on their lapels. Their media attacks liberals and social programs. The neo-con agenda was to push Syria out of Lebanon, change the government of Iran — again — conquer Iraq, and confront North Korea over their weapons program.

Psychopaths like secrecy. Psychopaths can be recognized for their ability to lie and rationalize their anti-social behavior. Why do some people want war? It made the vast fortunes of our "Robber Barons." Fear of an "outside enemy" panics people into giving up their liberty.

If our 'Jackals' failed, we used our military to protect economic imperialism abroad. The proxy war with communism was also about rubber, tin, and the potential oil deposits off the coast of Vietnam. Another factor was the access to illegal drugs, which provided massive profits.

There is another reason that other societies fear and hate us. We use their corrupt leaders to acquire their nation's resources. We did it in Indonesia, Africa, and Central and South America. We get them into debt and then practice economic Imperialism and then we send 'jackals', or the military, to preserve their economic interests — all at taxpayers' expense of course. No American company will lose a dime in Iraq or Syria; losses are insured by taxpayers.

There is a relationship between retail and wholesale killing. In our minds we sometimes separate national state killing from the psychopathic murderers we incarcerate and execute. Abused children, and abused nations, can become killers.

When governments start killing their own people, that is a symptom of the decay of the State. The deterioration of American political life has been a slow process since 1865. When governments break their own laws they are drifting toward dissolution. Rules are the social cement that holds a society together. Secrecy and denial have postponed the social conflict that is to come. The concept of 'no rules', courted by our dynastic elite families, invites social war. Let it be said here that social war against the republic, and the American people, began long ago. Maybe it began when conspirators murdered the man who tried to preserve the Union — Abraham Lincoln. He had two strikes against him. He was reportedly honest and wanted the government to print the 'greenbacks' to finance the war. President Kennedy also wanted to print government bonds for social programs. Apparently, the wealthy think that the printing of money by their banks should continue to indebt children, our grandchildren, and us. One time a man tried to teach the people how the financial game works. He created a game called "Monopoly." Who would not agree the crucial role of the banker in that game?

Bankers make money by keeping people and nations in debt. Wars cause massive debt, thus massive profits for the few. Printing currency makes wealth out of nothing and creates credit slaves. Every society needs a means to exchange goods ands services. Thomas Jefferson felt that by having private banks printing our currency, our liberties were at risk. Since 1913, and the passage of the Federal Reserve Act, private banks print the currency and control money supply. More significant is the fact that they set interest rates on every loan in the nation! They are not subject to election! The neo-cons did not raise taxes to fund their recent wars. They indebted you, and your children, and your grandchildren.

Chapter 12: Some Comments on Crime and the Society

Did you ever wonder why so much crime is displayed in the movies, the television, newspapers, and local news? Here are some interesting explanations: One viewpoint is that crime is dramatic and gets our attention. If you are walking down the street and witness assailants attacking others, or breaking property, or stealing, that misconduct alerts us to the threat — present to our own values — that has been implanted since early childhood. All societies have rules and laws that we conform to in order to have social peace. We are uneasy at seeing anyone commit crime. We are social animals and usually obey the rules, taboos, folkways, mores, customs, manners, city ordinances, and State laws that prescribe certain behaviors.

Most people are constructive and creative human beings, who work hard to support our families in a civil society. Parents, teachers, relatives, clergy, peer groups, and other institutions, teach us what is acceptable behavior. We depend on an orderly society to satisfy our basic needs and provide us with security and safety. We do not want to be victims of violence or have our property taken from us. Those that have reared us build a strong sense of justice into us. Those of us that have been abused and neglected have a higher incidence of anti-social criminal behavior than those who were well cared for by parents or guardians.

When we are confronted with the violation of our laws, we intervene, call the police, run away, or pretend we did not observe the infraction. Some people just become spectators, as there are different reactions to crime.

But, why is crime against persons, or property, viewed as entertainment? The ancient Greeks staged plays with comedy and tragedy for their citizens. The Romans adapted those 'shows' with a chorus that evolved into opera, and Americans developed movies and television. There is an important difference between the ancient Hellenes and our culture; the Greeks never portrayed violence on their stage. Why not? They did not show assault, murder, or war, because their children were present. A messenger might relate that Medea killed her children or that someone was destroyed in a war; however, outright violence was shielded from the young. Compare that to American cartoons that show violent acts. Even as young children, our population has been exposed to assaults and violence in our media, and you rarely see diplomacy, conflict resolution skills, tolerance, compromise, respect for others and regard for the value of human life. Good manners are neglected in the teaching of many young people.

Some psychologists offer the explanation that the audience of a crime drama experiences a satisfaction in viewing someone breaking the rules or laws. They posit that it provides a vicarious release for anti-social impulses that normal people have, but cannot express. This assumes people would like to get something for nothing when we watch others stealing, cheating, or hurting others without risking ourselves if we have suppressed anger. With some, there is an assumption that watching the infliction of pain or death in drama offers emotional satisfaction

Others would view the watching of violence as being morbid and sick. Most people are conforming and do not want to be ostracized, be a scapegoat or be punished. Some students of human behavior view this as sublimation, or a kind of wishful thinking, and rationalize that it is better to watch a violent fantasy than actually participate in a criminal act. In any case, to watch 'pretend' violence does not risk injury or death to the audience. It may make some appreciate social peace and the quality of their own lives. People who are not angry or hostile may prefer viewing the depiction of constructive lives and feel good movies and entertainments. Stories of love, romance, affection, and humor do enjoy popularity.

Another theory of media violence is this: It was found that during the World War II many of our boys and men could not kill the enemy. Thousands went into battles without firing their weapons or trying to kill the enemy. They attacked and risked their lives with their friends, but they did not kill. That should have been expected, as cultures teach their young not to hurt others, or kill. Their families, schools and churches taught them to value human life. People have to be taught fear and how to channel their anger before many of them will become violent and capable of killing. A drill sergeant telling his recruits that killing the enemy is not a revolting atrocity against the human race is not always effective in making him — or now her — into a killer.

It is possible that as a society becomes militarized and aggressive, the media takes on the propaganda role to mold young people to devalue human life. Enemies are demonized. This may be a partial explanation of why so much violence is fed to the American public. From an early age, our children have been brain washed by movies and TV programs to devalue other human beings. The video games show targets that are meant to frighten the game players. Threatened people are easily manipulated into attacking others if they feel endangered.

The social power of our industrial elite is based on private property, and our laws protect private property to the extent that some laws disregard human rights. Those who are deemed criminal lose many of their rights and often their freedom.

Some of the looters in New Orleans, after Katrina and the levee failures, should perhaps have been classified as survivors and not criminals. Yet the Federal government sent armed men rather than rescuers to help Katrina victims. Some owners were generous in aiding the thirsty, hungry, and homeless, and it is unknown how many desperate — normally law-abiding people — died from gunshot wounds. A disaster brings out the best in some and the worst in others.

In a disaster, some normal institutions break down. In New Orleans, some of the police drove off Cadillacs from a showroom that were going to be immersed in water. That was theft. Was it theft for hungry and thirsty people to break into an abandoned store for water and food? Some people died for lack of necessities, and the government did not send timely aid. Some researchers claim that it was planned neglect in New Orleans and they point out that FEMA did plan for, and provide aid to, Floridians whose Republican governor had a brother who was the President of the United States.

Most people aid other people in natural disasters. The mobs in New Orleans were desperate, trying to survive when they had been abandoned by governmental agencies on the County, State, and Federal level. Weather experts had forecasted potential disaster long before Katrina hit the area.

FEMA blocked the Red Cross effort to help survivors. FEMA was more concerned with martial law than saving lives. Was it incompetence or racism? Poor blacks suffered more than the well to do. It is probable that the white-collar criminals — who will rebuild their homes with taxpayer money — will do more fraud, and economic damage than the criminal looters or desperate survivors.

Some special interests showed more concern in rebuilding casinos than in helping the dispossessed poor. It may be a social crime to house people on land that is endangered by nature. Homes should not have been built in marshland near floodable lakes, deteriorating levees, and expanding canals. Maybe that city should move.

Lying, stealing, and killing, are considered as bad things to do in most societies. American society has a basic problem with our history. Our emigrant ancestors lied to the Native Americans and broke over 80 percent of our treaties by our successive legislatures and land stealing pioneers.

The invaders from Europe, and the Western movement, massacred whole tribes and villages, and fought the organized nations to forge the United States. Our ancestors miscalled these tribes Indians. They were actually a Stone Age people who were over run by an avaricious Iron Age people who were land hungry — a group of peasants who imposed their alien language, customs, religions, and laws, on the vanquished. Racist whites denied the first Americans the protection of American laws, and successive governments succumbed to predatory social policies. Some of the history books omitted the atrocities the Europeans and early whites committed against this lands original inhabitants. Yes, some of the tribes were cruel and brutal also, but that can hardly excuse the hypocrisy and murder by the so-called Christian settlers. Those unmentioned crimes remain a shame on our white washed history books.

Few realize that California was taken by Spain using violence and Catholic missionaries that enslaved Natives. Mexico took the land with a bloody revolution against Spain, and Mexico lost California, Nevada, Arizona, Colorado, New Mexico, Utah, and Texas in wars with the US. The rights of conquest established our economic system of Capitalism and private property.

Private legislatures, courts, and lawyers, establish property rights after the killing has stopped and peace is restored. Natural resources are apportioned, sold, inherited, and deeded, when social peace has been established. Lawyers do not create wealth, but they are useful in dividing up the land and resources to avoid anarchy, civil war, and social chaos. The legal systems, and courts, rely on fair laws that are acceptable to the general population. Courts are conflict resolution institutions and were rational creations of a society governed by laws. Even so, there is enough crime within this society to employ thousands of attorneys as prosecutors, and defense attorneys, to protect the innocent and rights of the guilty. Wars are social crimes known for the rampant destruction of property and the wasting of lives. It is a crime for those that make the weapons of war.

They are the merchants of death who profit and sometimes promote wars, in order to alter the political landscape, and expand their power.

The US Constitution gave common people the Bill of Rights and was a viable social compact until recently. Governments that violate their own constitution and laws invite replacement by elections or revolutions. Election fraud in two national elections is symptomatic of eventual political crisis. Most citizens still view themselves as sovereign and as living in a democratic republic. They are in for a big surprise.

Democracy is not a social myth to millions who were educated to believe in it. The disdain for violence has aided the stability of this nation, even as it is being polarized. By far the majority of citizens prefer war abroad as opposed to war at home. We live in a changing society that has surmounted Depression and the World War II. The brushfire wars are a serious problem as they militarize the state at the cost of social welfare, education, adequate medical care for all, and the desire for peace. In the past, our elected representatives adapted our laws to fit a changing society. The current problem is that most of the population did not select the candidates, and we have minority rule by an Industrial elite who no longer respect — nor fear — the people. Some of our elite call common people, "useless mouths."

It took generations for common people to achieve rights for children, women, slaves, Native Americans, and minorities. We no longer rely on Prophets, Popes, Bishops, Priests, Mullahs and Ministers for codes and laws written by gods. We are a secular society even though we are bombarded by fundamentalist right-wing propaganda. There were too many divergent religions to create a state religion.

People in this world are punished for a crime even though the punishment does not stop crime. Social laws have replaced the religious concept of sin; people are no longer punished for sin.

Society is not totally rational; it is easy to see some ways to improve the system. A full employment policy would reduce crime. Better education programs might also be beneficial as opportunities are not equal because funding is unequal. Child abuse and neglect contribute to violence, as well as social discrimination. Society puts too much stress on competition rather than on social cooperation.

Programming for failure begins in the first grade. Each child has needs that cannot be ignored by society without great cost. They are the future of the society and every one should have decent housing, food, clothes, and medical care. General welfare can be supported by taxes! It is in the Declaration of Independence!

White-collar criminals and corporate crime have not been given the attention that it deserves. Americans dislike privilege, and someday will redress the imbalance of power that gave human rights to entities that can be killed with legislation. The slave trade was once tolerated in our divided society; it took a war to remove it.

The very definition of crime has changed with time; it is not an absolute word. During the Dark Ages, a five-year-old was executed in England for theft. Today, the execution — and not the theft — would be defined as crime.

It is time we took a closer look at crime: Better education for all children, and a full employment policy for all able adults, would reduce property crime. Many people in jail need to be released and provided with care, such as the mentally ill and addicts. They require hospitals clinics and employment opportunities. Many people in business, and in the government, need investigation and trials. The justice system takes too long to operate. It is also ridiculous to fine poor people who do not have money to pay their fines. Perhaps I am radical to suggest that corporations that break our laws should be seized and operated to diminish our national debts. Why not put the crooked corporations in receivership and operate them for the public good? You can guess that I am fed up with corporate property rights that ignore some human rights. If capitalism were truly regulated by government it would require an honest government.

Other nations will continue to fear and disrespect our society, unless we investigate, indict, prosecute, and abide, by social rule.

CHAPTER 13: HOW TO DESTROY A CIVILIZATION — OURS

The first ingredient for self-destruction is to make weapons for the destruction of future "enemies." The United States did this with the construction of over twenty-five thousand nuclear weapons. Because of this, other nations have made weapons that can destroy whole population centers.

Russia, England, France, China, South Africa, Israel, Pakistan, India, North Korea, and Iran, have followed our example and have made weapons that will eliminate millions of people, if used. Our behavior has spawned a new arms race; in this, and perhaps this alone, Al Qaeda wants to be like us! They, and others, want WMDS. Today, the Saudi Kingdom wants nuclear technology to match Iran because it fears Iran as a rival.

These weapons have not given us security but instead have threatened whole civilizations. Now we face biological and chemical weapons as well. Maybe we should have just made nuclear hand grenades. The United States is a terrorist organization. Hatred is the flower that grows in the garden of fear. Other nations in the world hate bullies and they hate this nation that maintains weapons that threaten civilizations.

Our social institutions are lagging far behind our weapons scientists. When we engage in ideological or resource wars, we risk a general conflagration. What is there to stop fundamentalist true believers from setting off weapons of mass destruction in third party nations, and just standing by as they destroy their societies? The nations need to cooperate if they are to prevent terrorist cells from instigating future wars. Our current policies create more Osama bin Ladens, even as we kill more Iraqi citizens. We are now the world's problem society because we abandoned fundamental principles of human decency. A half of Iraq's population is children; they will remember "Shock and Awe." An economic and political war will become a religious and racial war. Civil war in Iraq continues with conflicts between Kurds, Sunnis and Shiites, and our forces who cannot tell which side we're on.

We will continue to waste our youth, empty our national treasury, and indebt our future generations, as long as we harbor the illusion that we are a super power, maintain hundreds of overseas bases, and threaten others in order to control natural resources like the oil in Iraq and the (projected) natural gas pipeline in Afghanistan.

The neocons make more enemies every day with their shortsighted aggressive policies. In addition to this, they have removed our liberties through the Patriot Act. The national media is no longer reliable for giving us the facts. Democracy disappeared with purchased government, corporate sponsored legislators, lobbyism, tax-exempt trust foundations, public relations companies, militarism, and rogue oil corporations.

I used to think that the Catholic Church was a conservative institution that historically allied itself with monarchists, aristocrats, and economic elites against the general population. I was surprised to learn that Pope John II had discovered that 80% of Catholics, in the Americas, were poor. He feared the spread of Castroism and redirected the efforts of the Church with a series of social programs. It was my understanding that priests and nuns engaged in clean water projects, sanitation programs, educational efforts, health activities, and social reforms to prevent radicalism and violence. I heard that the Church even gave some land to the poorest. These social programs were viewed with hostility by the elites and these reformers were labeled as "Red Priests." Over 800 priests were killed by death squads. Corrupt governments in Mexico, and Central and South America have murdered nuns, and even a bishop and cardinal. This has been going on for decades as the Catholic Church tries to aid the poor.

How does this concern the United States? We have intervened in this hemisphere's politics ever since the Monroe Doctrine. We sent our troops into the Caribbean and Central America on numerous occasions as we practiced "dollar diplomacy" and supported regimes that were not democratic. We loaned their elites money, extracted resources from our neighbors cheaply, and sold them manufactured goods to guarantee profits for our businessmen. We trained terrorist Special Forces and overthrew sitting governments for our own interests.

Our numerous interventions were resented. We were the "Colossus of the North," and recently some of those Southern neighbors have begun trying to regain control over their own natural resources. Several countries have now opted for leftist governments as they try to re-negotiate contracts with American business interests. Our CIA tried to overthrow Chavez in Venezuela as the people supported their leader who has used oil profits for social programs. The CIA redoubled its efforts and the country is now on the rocks due to economic warfare.

American torture, and the killing of prisoners in Afghanistan and Iraq, is not a recent phenomenon. The poisoning of village wells and the throwing of prisoners out of helicopters in Vietnam — and other atrocities by "Tiger Units" and "Phoenix Programs" — are all indications of the barbarism that has infected our military and intelligence operations, which have all been shielded from the public by "national secrecy." National secrets hide national crimes.

The torture in prisons, run by the United States, is just the tip of an iceberg; this nation lost its moral compass decades ago. Unknown crimes remain uncorrected. Panamanian National Guardsmen were killed with pistol shots to their head while their hands were tied with plastic handcuffs behind their backs. Around twelve mass graves were found in Panama after the Reagan/Bush invasion. The Republicans wanted to regain control of the Panama Canal with a new treaty — a new puppet government of Panama seemed to be the goal. The dead in that invasion were estimated to be around five thousand Panamanians. Of course, both Torrijoes, and his successor Manuel Noriega, were former CIA assets.

Assassination and war removed Panamanian leaders. No American media showed the slain National Guardsmen. Shooting helpless prisoners is criminal. The poorer sections of Panama City were bombed and set on fire. Americans can live with that because most of us never knew what was going on to eliminate the "drug dealer" who was, in fact, partnered with our CIA with arms deals, for secret wars against the "Reds," in Central and

South America. Perhaps he wanted a bigger cut from the rug and arms smuggling, and they just got rid of him.

Phil Agee, a former CIA agent, exposed every agent in Mexico through to Tierra del Fuego. He was motivated to expose the harm they were doing in that hemisphere. The CIA hounded their former agent out of several European nations, and he finally fled to Cuba for sanctuary. Someone reportedly sent Agee a bomb in a typewriter. That is how whistle-blowers are rewarded.

Agee tried to alert citizens about the illegality, malfeasance, and corruption of some CIA cells. Other agents have also written books on the CIA. Many CIA people are honest and worked hard for the government, not knowing about the assassinations, blackmail, torturing prisoners of war, kidnapping, drug smuggling, and the compromising of our own. Some were "Good Germans" who knew but would not speak out against the team.

Even members of the CIA considered Congressional oversight of the secret agency a joke. Some allege that spying on other branches of our own government took place. Secrets inside of secrets have led to this sad state of affairs in our shadow government. Some members of the agency are guilty of propaganda, destroying evidence, lying to Congress, and withholding information. Prevarication has become an art form. Who would ever want to work for an agency that might frame them or kill them? Bluntly stated, a supra legal operation by a member of the intelligence agency is an illegal act.

Institutional law breaking is a threat to our Constitution and Liberties. Agency members, enmeshed in crimes, will be a serious problem to this society. Countries need intelligence agencies to know what is going on in the world. It is not feasible to burn down the house to get rid of the rats; you should not throw the baby out with the bath water. Reformation of the CIA would be as delicate as removing cancer tumors from a brain. Some purged agents went to work for private corporations. That too, deserves some examination — especially if they were "jackals."

CIA Director Colby drowned in a river behind his house. Some thought he was a traitor for revealing agency malfeasance to the Frank Church Committee. When Colby's wife viewed his body, she asked, "Where is his life jacket? He never went on the river without a life jacket."

Chapter 15: American Lemmings on the March

The neo-conservative plans were aired on national public radio and one has to wonder how much of it was an April Fools prank. William Kristol revealed that the Iraqi invasion was part of the plan to "introduce democracy in the Middle East." Democracy is a luxury that can only work in societies with a certain level of general education, a minimal level of development, and a certain level of social cohesion. Democracy is not what is needed in a bombed-out, illiterate nation where a civil war has been exacerbated by foreign fighters. To suggest such a thing is a cruel joke.

Meanwhile, our own elections are more and more suspicious. The American Enterprise Institute and the American Century have openly stated the following goals for the United States: To continue to build a Military that is unchallengeable by any other society; to carry out pre-emptive attacks on nations that may pose a future threat; to replace other governments in the Middle East, by force if necessary; and to ignore the World Court, and the United Nations, in pursuit of our own national goals.

Iran, Syria, North Korea, and even Saudi Arabia will be confronted, because the elites believe they have the power to engage these regimes. Our government never mentions the nuclear weapons given by Kazakhstan to Iran. Every threatened government will engage in acquiring nuclear weapons to defend themselves against our intervention and domination. The neo-conservative doctrine will probably embroil us in regional wars and such wars risk expansion. The science of destruction is way ahead of sound diplomacy by our ideological leaders.

Millions should be out in our streets, and on phones, at least trying to avoid this planned catastrophe. Think how Americans would react if a foreign culture bombed the electrical grid, water treatment plants, killed innocent civilians that lived near communication centers, destroyed and scattered our armed forces, and said they were bringing democracy and freedom to us. Of course, the bravest would resist and defy occupation. A war against civilians is fought differently from a war against uniformed military. Each civilian casualty strengthens the population's desire to resist. We would hope our people would then have the guts to follow a leader over the cliffs and into the sea.

War will not create a world government, or era, in which corporate power replaces nation states. Our elite will not be able to privatize the world's resources at the expense of weaker nations. When Colin Powell had to give a speech at the United Nations in which he rationalized our unilateral action in attacking Iraq, he was met with a stunned and disapproving silence. The international diplomatic tide turned against this nation during that speech.

The United Nations, however, was not able to preserve peace.

Our nation is in debt thanks to the war hawks that voters should have tossed out of office. Maybe some of them deserve indictment for supporting destructive policies. If Congress did their job, we would not be engaged in wars decreed on Presidential orders. You do not see the Swedes attacking other nations and trying to dominate the world. Peace is not bad for the health of a nation. On the other hand, if psychopaths are in office they can do great harm.

This nation cannot remain founded on lies; truths are the remedy. The world is real, and fact-finding is crucial for your survival.

CHAPTER 16: A PROBATION REPORT IS BASED ON AVAILABLE RECORDS AND HEARSAY...

The 25,000 weapons of mass destruction that we own are available to one man — the President. How reliable are the presidents we have had lately? George W. Bush had a record of drunk driving and, as Texas Governor, he executed mentally ill and retarded criminals! Obama was given the Nobel Peace Prize, apparently in anticipation of something; but he went on to start wars himself. This does not inspire confidence.

Saddam did not have WMDs, but we do, thanks to a craven Congress. They are hidden away in silos, bunkers on ships, and in the bowels of submarines that prowl the world's seas. They have been created by an insane industrial society. What led us to stockpile weapons that could destroy civilizations in hours? Fear and distrust may have played a part in creating the means for the destruction of enemies, and eventually us.

Some propagandist said nuclear weapons were deterrents to war! Well, I am sure you can recall the Korean War, the Vietnamese War, the Dominican Republic intervention, Grenada/Panama, Lebanon, the Gulf Wars, War in the Congo, Middle Eastern Wars, India and Pakistan Wars, the China/India war, the Falkland War, the Suez Canal War, Chechnya, Rwanda, Angola, Afghanistan, Libya, Iraq and Syria. Weapons did not stop war.

War profiteers still prosper by making these weapons as population are living in fear. There are some conflicts not remembered, like Indonesia and Guatemala. No — genocidal weapons do not make anyone more secure. Wars have not been prevented. There were many civil wars in the colonies when the major empires broke up. I do not believe that the nation state protects us today. In fact, I believe that our present government is the greatest threat to humanity since Genghis Khan, Alexander, Napoleon, Mussolini, and Adolf Hitler. Those leaders did not have nuclear weapons, missiles, and bacterial and chemical weapons.

Democracy is not an exportable governmental system unless people are willing to accept it. Democracy comes from the people, and cannot be imposed. Our brand of Capitalism is also being resisted.

This society lost democracy in America a long time ago. Currently, we have indirect plutocracy. Most eligible Americans voters do not vote. There are few differences between the two major parties. Where is the peace candidate who believes in diplomacy? Most Americans now know that Congress does not represent them. We have special interest government managed by a small dynastic elite that funds both parties to hedge their bets. Lobbyism killed the Republic that we still had in the era of small farmers. When President Andrew Jackson was in the White House, the Congress more accurately resembled the American people. We sent common people to Washington to address common needs. General US Grant, and his presidency, was the start of crony capitalism. President Jackson did not trust, nor like, corporations; he thought they would be bad for the country.

Today, a half of the Senators are millionaires. What do they do for our unemployed or homeless people? Corporations eliminated each other and created semi monopolies. The creation of massive piles of wealth by a dynastic elite enabled the few to translate their economic power into political power. Sponsored candidates do not solve the nations' social problems.

The numbers of so-called representatives of the people are few in Congress and at the State level. Some Congressmen are sponsored, owned and operated by banks, insurance companies, energy companies, military contractors, drug companies, heavy industry, and chemical companies; and those corporations are controlled and managed by the dynastic power elite families. Big money has created an unbalanced society. They maintain power indirectly and hide in the shadows of history. They would even deny that they exercise such social power over our lives.

Special interests are propagandizing us. Repeated lies are mistaken for facts. That is what spin is all about. The airwaves have been taken over by private companies for private profit. Special people who have the privilege of great wealth have filtered the information given to our society. The people are constantly being under informed about what is happening in our society and what occurs abroad. Our danger is in the fact that many believe the lies of business and government officials. We have underestimated the social impact of advertising.

One percent of citizens control 40% of the wealth. Foundations provide 38% of newspaper stories! The public is constantly being entertained, distracted, frightened, and propagandized by media funded by narrow interests. The media has been covering up drastic policies.

American governments have assassinated foreign leaders of sovereign nations. We have overthrown governments, bribed governments, and even threatened some with nuclear annihilation. The United States is a bad world citizen, and that is why we are hated and disliked all over the planet. Basically, we have frightened the world and lost allies that we had for over a hundred years. This mis-government could cost us millions of lives with its aggressive policies. Meanwhile, we still have unemployment, crime pollution, a deteriorating infra structure, and a tax structure that has over one thousand millionaires — and a few billionaires — not paying a dime in Federal taxes! Can we really afford these trust fund babies?

Have you read how Lyndon B. Johnson killed John F. Kennedy? He had a great deal of help. He was used by a cabal. Lyndon Johnson's personal attorney wrote a book on it. (Bob Schieffer says the book is a pack of lies; maybe some details are off-base. Some of it may be true.) In his dying days, President Johnson confessed to two of his attorneys. Did a contrite L.B.J. want the true story to come out, or did he want to throw us off the sent with yet another alternative story? Johnson provided secret service badges for the plotters; this may explain why local police did not pick up some suspects.

Johnson allegedly became involved over the Bobby Baker and Billy Sol Estes scandals. There was also a murder to conceal a stolen Texas election). For several years, Lyndon Johnson and J. Edgar Hoover walked their dogs together in the mornings, and that is when the FBI director decided to help Vice President Johnson by controlling the investigation in Texas. Apparently, lobbyism threatened Lyndon Johnson. J. Edgar Hoover had a long-term friendship with Clint Murchison Jr. and they vacationed together and gambled at the Santa Anita racetrack together. The friends also spent time in Las Vegas Hotels. (The Mafia had interests in Santa Anita, as well as Las Vegas, casinos and hotels. Meyer Lansky (Mafia) had a compromising photo of Clyde Tolson and Hoover. That enabled Frank Costello — the Mafia leader — to blackmail the famous law enforcement officer. The agreement was that the Mafia would not extort, rob banks, or kidnap. That would embarrass the FBI who investigated those Federal crimes. In exchange, J. Edgar Hoover would not investigate mafia gambling, prostitution, the numbers racket, or their racetrack operations. He would give organized crime a pass to operate the sin economy. To seal the deal, Frank Costello gave J. Edgar Hoover his own hitman.

Sirhan-Sirhan, named as the assassin of Bobby Kennedy, worked at Santa Anita racetrack, cleaning stables. Sirhan had a two-month memory loss. He is still doing time. That assassination investigation also had a cloud over it, and witnesses were threatened, regarding what they had seen — by the police.

There were also too many shots and bullet holes for there to have only been one man firing a weapon. Regarding the Jack Kennedy killing, witnesses claimed to have heard eight shots; the press also reported that number — an improbable number for one bolt-action rifle.

Ed Clark, an attorney, was one of the conspirators for the assassination of Jack Kennedy. He employed Mac Wallace as one of the assassins. Richard Nixon and Lyndon Johnson were in the Murchison house the night before the assassination of Jack Kennedy, along with other notables like J. Edgar Hoover and oil people, When the Vice President came out of the meeting, he was overheard to have said to 'Lady Bird' Johnson, "The Kennedys will never embarrass me again."

The Secret service had a late night drinking time the night before the President was killed. They were not on their toes; no military units were called out to guard the parade route. The next day, Kennedy was dead. Hoover covered it up. Richard Milhous Nixon, the Clint Murchison family, and J. Edgar Hoover, were all involved. In all probability, the CIA- and some military — were also complicit. Allen Dulles arranged the cover-up and he, and his cohorts, may have actually been involved in killing Kennedy, and over fifty witnesses afterwards.

According to Lyndon Johnson's Attorney, Johnson feared perdition. The national TV networks, as usual, are covering up this national tragedy. Most of the American people realize that there was a real conspiracy, yet the national media spews out the propaganda line to protect Texas Oil billionaires who paid six million dollars for the murder. The FBI/CIA covered it up so that J. Edgar Hoover could continue as director and the CIA avoided being broken up by the Kennedy's. Allen Dulles, who was fired by Kennedy, was on the lying Warren Commission! Boggs — a commission member — had an air accident.

The CIA has been full of ardent fanatical anti-communists for years, and some are loyal to private interests, but not the American people. It is a big bureaucracy, which is compartmentalized. Most are honest people, but they have had secret departments that break laws. They are a nest of garter snakes, gopher snakes, and king snakes, and here and there you will find vipers.

The real patriots warned this nation about shadow government making policies. Black operations are not accountable to Congress, or even to the Presidency (Deniability factor). This is a true Machiavellian tactic.

If a CIA agent commits a crime, he or she can be easily controlled by the agency. Besides signing the secrecy act, he or she can be prosecuted or blackmailed. Silence is paramount. Blackmail can be a two-edged sword. According to Lt. Commander Al Martin, there are Federal judges that belong to the CIA and therefore potential whistle-blowers would not find a neutral judicial system. Agents can be framed, or indicted. Spies are trained to be burglars. That gives the institution leverage over its members.

There have been hundreds of books written on the Kennedy assassination that muddy up the waters; some are probably limited hangout books with partial truths and false trails. There have been good independent investigations that show the Warren Commission Report was a cover-up to protect the guilty. The sealing of records for 75 years was to avoid a revolution. That cover-up gained cooperation of many branches of the law enforcement on the threat of foreign involvement and risk of nuclear war. The "patsy," Lee Harvey Oswald, had defected to Soviet Russia and had married a girl whose father was a Soviet intelligence officer.

How was he able to come back to the US so easily? Who was working with him?

In the Kennedy cover up, law enforcement aided in limiting investigations, and cooperating with the cover-up, on the rationale of national interest. There is strong evidence, uncovered by independent investigation, that the FBI and the CIA got a chance to investigate themselves. An American MID (Army) agent sent a registered letter to the FBI Director informing him of the plot to kill Kennedy (the Mafia tapes intercepted in Florida by the FBI, indicated that President Kennedy "is going to be hit ").

The KGB sent a small file on Oswald after the assassination. After the Cold War was over, it was revealed by the Russians that their real file on Lee Harvey Oswald was a stack two feet tall. It was also reported that the father of his Russian wife — Marina Oswald Porter — was a General in the KGB. According to one report, every female that Oswald slept with in Russia was a member of the KGB. He was closely watched, thought to be an American spy.

Here is another small piece of information: Under the Kennedys, and other presidents, multiple assassination plots were mounted against Fidel Castro. Now, there is some speculation that Santos Trafficante tipped Fidel Castro off. The CIA collaborated with the Mob. All the plots failed. Castro had generously let Sam Trafficante out of a Cuban Jail.

CHAPTER 17: MORE THAN THE MIND CAN BEAR

It's not a simple task to understand how we got to our present condition. In 1953, this society had troops in Korea dealing out death to over a million people. We lost over fifty thousand boys and men. The Reds had invaded a divided Korea, and President Truman had organized a U.N. coalition to answer violence with war. My classes had GI veterans in them and I worked nights with ex-military who were funded by the GI Bill, and shot-up veterans were a common sight hobbling around the campus.

To this day most Americans do not know that our side used germ warfare during the Korean War. A returning American P.O.W. was tortured to death in an effort to conceal our act of total war. Brainwashing by them was answered with brainwashing by the CIA. One conscience-bound CIA agent who objected to torturing our own people was drugged with LSD, hit on the head, and tossed out of a window in New York.

The method had been used in Czechoslovakia and in Germany. The CIA adopted the same tactics and even produced a manual on how to perform such "suicides," or "accidents." In essence, the intelligence agency became just as immoral as we claim our enemies to be.

I recall a Mr. Goleman, a teacher of mine. He was a mild mannered man with a mustache who wore tweed clothes. He passed out our first reading to the class of Stockton College freshpeople. One of the very first things he said to the class was, "I will try to love you." He had a small smile, but there was a hint of some doubt as to whether we were truly loveable. A young man who had his arm around a girl was continuing a conversation as our teacher spoke. This occurred in the first two minutes of class. Mr. Goleman addressed the amorous student and asked him to leave the class. He said he would fail the course and therefore it would be better to leave straightaway. The young man got up and left with the little dignity that he was afforded. By reputation, and later performance, this was one of the greatest teachers that I was ever to encounter. He used the Socratic method of asking numerous questions that led to thinking, rather than sponging.

We started studying mythology and went on to study the literature of other civilizations. We eventually encountered Herodotus, Thucydides, Oswald Spengler, and Arnold Toynbee who wrote about the Decline and Death of Civilizations. We discussed what state our civilization was in at that time. Mr. Goleman believed that we were in an era of Decline. I did not accept that notion at the time. I got Will Cuppy's book *The Decline and Fall of Almost Everybody* and laughed at the humorist's jab at history, and the pessimists. I can no longer laugh about what has happened in America.

We are going to install lasers in space and into satellites; the goal is to dominate the whole planet. While we close bases here, over seven hundred bases overseas must surely reveal, to even the most under informed citizen, that our dynastic elite families are practicing economic imperialism. Our dynastic elite families practice technological militarism at the taxpayers' expense. Their goal is to privatize the world's human and natural resources: to won them.

Our advanced technological power has corrupted some of our politicians, and some of our military. The scientific edge we used to possess has our ideological extremists drunk with power. They don't even notice that the Russians and Chinese are outstripping us in the fields of science and engineering.

Look at our abandonment of diplomacy and lack of allies. This country cannot reform itself fast enough to save itself from future disasters. Congress abandoned the people when they gave a single man the power to wage war.

Of seven major industrial nations, we are the only one without a workable national health care system. Twenty million Americans have inadequate health care or none at all. Education and health care have been badly neglected for a nation that boasts of its wealth. Too many of our children are born into poverty. Our future has been risked by neo-conservatism, which is really reactionary.

Parson Malthus declared the following as ways to control human population on this planet: Famine, war, and disease. He recognized that birth rates increase at a rate to surpass the food supply. The population has exploded in the last 100 years and is still increasing exponentially, mainly among the least educated and least able to feed themselves.

And this, despite the fact that millions of people are being killed in wars, and civil wars. The increased food production that came with better technology has been a boost, although in many areas the water table is getting low and more and more chemical fertilizer is needed; this may not go on forever. Better sanitation and medical practices have extended life in some cultures; while others have had higher death rates.

The weapon-ization of small pox and anthrax, by our military, is an ominous sign that genocide may be on the table. Such bacteriological weapons are not military weapons. They are not logical weapons against enemy troops, naval forces, or airmen. Those are weapons that kill babies, children, and adults of every age. These are genocidal weapons that are ideal for eugenicists and race lunatics.

Before we moved in with bases in the Middle East and Central Asian heartland, the American policy was organized to weaken both Iraq and Iran. Islamic terrorists were trained by the British and US armed forces, originally to fight against the Soviet Union in Afghanistan and the Soviet Central Asian republics. But the Muhajadeen later turned on us. This is called "blowback."

We did not rebuild Afghanistan and subsequently it became a land that harbored terrorists, and produced poppies for drugs. What have we now achieved? Well, the CIA has a lucrative drug business that undermines Russia and Europe, that's one thing. More civil war and a guerilla war will last for decades. The Taliban will target any schools and hospitals that we build in Afghanistan. We failed to win the peace by not rebuilding what we destroyed, by targeting civilians, and by creating a wasteland through war. We did the same in Libya. We are doing the same in Syria.

Governmental whistle-blowers tried to protect our society. The media failed us like the Justice Department failed to do its job. Notice that today, while whistle-blowers are charged with crimes, criminal politicians remain in office not having been investigated. Past administrations are not indicted. Past administrations are not prosecuted for breaking our laws, and international laws.

In the economic sphere, some of our banks are too big to fail. Iceland threw some of their bankers in prison. The Netherlands nationalized some of their banks. The Hungarian government ejected the 400-year-old Rothschild family out of their country. Notice a lack of information in your news. Reuters, Haves, and Wolf news networks were founded by, or have connections with, that socially powerful banking dynasty.

Notice the European coalition governments. Part of their financial crisis is government debt to the private banks. Did not the Rothschilds favor a single world currency at the Council of Vienna? Previous civilizations were based on gold, silver, and copper. Today, private institutions print fiat money with nothing of value to back it up; and they set interest rates for all debts. This is both government debt and private debt.

Bankers control the money supply. Bankers are above election. This is insane.

Chapter 18: Some Comments on Written and Oral History

I was a teacher at a school in Humboldt County. We were given four sample history books to choose from for our fourth grade classes. One California textbook was objectionable because it hid the truth and contained a blatant omission. It did mention that California natives had inhabited the area within our villages for tens of thousands of years. It did mention the fact that the Spanish came over and claimed the land for the King of Spain, and established Catholic Missions along the Coast. It did not, however, mention that Indians were killed by soldiers, and sailors, before the Missions were built, in order to "save their souls" while making slaves of the survivors. It included information about the Russians who established a fort at Fort Ross, and how they became engaged in harvesting sea otters. The book also covered the fact that Mexico rebelled against the European king, and the territory concerned became part of Mexico. It mentioned the US war against Mexico that netted us the rich territory of California in a peace settlement, but it did not go into detail about the violence. War was barely mentioned.

No need to disturb young minds with the fact that America expanded by killing people and taking land from others. The watered down book said that Californian Indians died from disease and simply "disappeared." I learned from a school board member how her husband's ancestors massacred the Mattole River Indians. It is true that 4,000 Indians did die near the San Jose Mission. Many succumbed to smallpox, tuberculosis, and other diseases because they lacked immunity from the invaders ailments. The book did not mention the 40,000 natives who were murdered by white settlers who took their land. There was not much mentioned about the mis-named Indians who fought brief conflicts with Stone Age weapons against Iron Age people armed with swords, guns, and cannons.

Early settlers were fearful of the Indians, who for some odd reason were distrustful of these new arrivals with guns. The settlers had a stockade built around their own house. When members of the Squaw Creek village found a cow stuck in a creek and butchered it for food, a small number of whites attacked the village while the men and boys were at the beach gathering barnacles, mussels and other shellfish. Reportedly, there were only five or six whites but they were heavily armed with rifles, shotguns, pistols and knives. They attacked the old men and the little boys in the campsite first, and then killed the women. After that, they went into the brush to kill the children. My informant said they ran out of bullets and resorted to using knives and pistol butts on the children. One rancher grabbed a baby by his heel and was going to hit the child when he noticed that the little boy had six toes on each foot. That particular child was spared and later raised by the whites. He reportedly lived well into his seventies, and then disappeared into the mountains one day and never came back.

When the massacre occurred, word was sent to other ranchers along the river of the "Indian War." Other whites joined the killers and they ambushed the village men as they came back from the Lagoon, scattering the survivors. Word went to Eureka, and later to San Francisco. Units of the Army were dispatched and they took surviving Mattole Indians to Covelo. In this instance, the Army rescued rather than killed the native Californians. But there were similar incidents all over California; these killings were mentioned in local newspapers. A Stanford professor documented the murder of over forty thousand original inhabitants. In the grab for land, the murder of Indians has been omitted from history books; they have been used as instruments of propaganda.

Violence was a part of every change in the rush for ownership of California. Control of the land, or its ownership, went from Indian Villages to Spain, then to Mexico, and then to the Americans. Private property rights! Private property rights are determined after the killing is over, and peace breaks out.

The winners in conflict determine the new rules of societies. Private property is sold, deeded, traded, and acquired after the killing has stopped and peace is restored; lawyers and courts appear after the blood stops flowing. Very few people know that capitalism, or the free enterprise system, begins with war — killing. If they were born in peaceful times, the citizens do not connect their current economic activity with historical conflicts between villages, tribes, nations, and empires. Religious Christians view stealing, lying, and killing as basic prohibitions; but compartmentalized thinking enables them to maintain beliefs that do not condemn this when committed by "authorities."

We were not delivered to our parents by a stork, or discovered in a cabbage patch. The thousands of goddesses and gods cannot have sole access to the absolute truth, because there is disagreement as to what constitutes the truth. Rights to rule are not a divine gift of a goddess. We live in a natural world that has some value to us, and we are valuable and the measure of all things, according to our beliefs. Disregarding our natural environment will eventually kill us through pollution and through waste of necessary resources. Native peoples respected the world and did less damage to the earth.

Repeated untruths are accepted by the gullible as fact. Do you really believe that Atlas holds the world on his shoulders? Or do we think that the world is on the back of a turtle? Apparently, some elites still believe that one race is designated to rule over all other peoples.

Human behavior depends on real information. People need to know the facts and realize what is not real. Illusions have a tendency to cause great grief to our species.

The Catholic Church has one of the oldest bureaucracies in the Western World. The Protestant Reformation led to hundreds of years of religious wars. Now, while Catholics had to support their own separate schools if they wanted to teach religion during the week, Protestant fundamentalists are trying to bring religion back into the schools. They do not appreciate the genius of our founding fathers that separated religion from the state. People kill each other's bodies, claiming they think they are saving each other's souls. They kill over territory and archaic ideas and they usually rationalize and excuse their destructive, criminal behavior. But only toleration, understanding, and cooperation enable people to live together in peace.

The founding fathers of the nation advocated religious toleration. That still may be a good idea that ignorant Christians should consider. Consider this: In feudal times, the Catholic Church had great power. At one time, the Pope abolished all debts — he took that action every seven years. Usury was a sin in the eyes of the Church.

Chapter 19: Our Story: Social Comments on Past Empires—and California

Today, power comes out of the barrel of right-wing black box voting machines manufactured by Billionaire Brothers who tried to corral the silver market. Silver became valuable as a conductor in our missiles and almost disappeared in our coinage. That may have been the reason the Hunt brothers wanted a monopoly on silver. They may have been players in the oil business. Nevada was the silver state, but most of my comments will be about the Golden State (which also had some oil ... that is currently being depleted).

California is known as the Golden State; it grew with the Gold Rush that led to a mass of immigrants entering the State, which was newly taken from Mexico in the Treaty of Guadalupe. With Silicon Valley, California now has about the sixth largest economy in the world, with technology replacing food production as top earner, and gold as the major asset. The State exemplified rapid social and economic changes. It is a lighthouse state, and what occurs here is often repeated in other parts of the nation. Two world wars, and the Dust Bowl Migration of the 1930s, increased its population. The population was around 6 million in the 1940s and is over 39 million today. It supplanted New York and Pennsylvania, which used to be the most populated.

The state prospered and advanced under Republican Governor Earl Warren, providing a time when we had good schools and a fine higher education system of Junior Colleges, State Colleges, and the Universities of UCLA and Cal at Berkeley. Stanford, a private university, produced the brains that started Silicon Valley. Some school districts were rich and others were poor. What we spent on our children declined with our student test scores. Educational opportunity was not equal to all, and infrastructure was allowed to deteriorate. The Californian correctional facilities, and the California Youth Authority, were once considered the most progressive in the country. Other states came to inspect and borrow from the State mental hygiene system incorporated there (state hospitals).

Rapid growth and the successive Conservative Republican and Democratic State House, allowed the deterioration of public services. During one democratic regime they built 11 new prisons and one new university. Social progress did not keep up with the growth. Tight-fisted Republicans, and Conservative Democrats, closed the State mental hospitals and tossed the mentally ill back into the counties — of course, those programs were underfunded and homelessness increased in the state.

In the 1960s, California was a beacon of sunshine, youth, liberal attitudes and the mantra of "love and peace." It carried this aura for many years, but in fact the seeds of destruction were planted precisely then.

Ronald Reagan (Governor 1967–75) may have thought he was saving money, but California suddenly had an increase in serial murderers. De Witt state hospital was closed. Juan Corona, a former patient at De Witt, killed over forty farm workers and buried them in fruit orchards in Northern California. Juan, and his brother, employed the workers and then murdered them rather than paying them for work done. More 'scrupulous' Californian and Texan farmers and ranchers would employ the Mexican workers and then, without paying them, would call the Border Patrol to come and deport the workers who had no legal protection in the situation; the greedy exploited the needy. It took decades to get portable toilets and water for the migrant workers. Their wages were low because the Wagner Act did not allow them to collectively bargain for decades.

Now to return to earlier history: Some Californian textbooks mention the man Ishi — the last of his tribe. Ishi was discovered in Northern California. They way he thought whites were sometimes like children and he thought our invention of glue and piped water were useful. But, the books did not mention that posses hunted the Indians. That is how the area of Yosemite National Park was discovered. The Indians lost their homes for the creation of a national park that is visited by millions of tourists today. At one time, Disney wanted a piece of the action at Yosemite, but the Sierra Club — and other conservation groups — fought its commercialization.

Now, to go way back in the history of the United States: Our legal system was emplaced after the killing and stealing stopped. Spain used violence to take California. In Baja California, the natives were greeted with cannons firing glass, metal fragments, and lead. Spain lost her colony to Mexico in a revolutionary war when Father Hidalgo rang the Church bell, called the people together and repeated grievances and incited war. Father Hidalgo wanted Mexico to develop her own industries, like the farming of caterpillars to start a silk industry. Spain was only interested in mercantilism, extracting mineral wealth and protecting home industries.

In the growing United States, 'Manifest Destiny' was a euphemism for imperialism. The United States took California away from Mexico in a war. Mexico had to give up more than Texas and California to get American troops out of Mexico City. Arizona, New Mexico, Utah, Colorado, and Nevada were invaded and taken through war. President Polk was passionate about acquiring new territory.

Lawyers in legislatures and courts establish private property rights when wars subside. The free enterprise system is founded on murder and theft. Few, if any, economics books mention that capitalism was established through force and violence. Only through social peace are property, land, and resources sold, traded, taxed or deeded. Social property is that which is held as common land, public land, property owned by governments like cities, and County and State property. You would not be able to walk, drive, or move anywhere without social property or public paths, roads, and freeways. In the earliest stages of imperialistic societies, property rights superseded human rights. Only when peace has been established do we see cooperation and the lessening of deadly competition for land resources and social power.

During the Gold Rush in 1849, one of the first things the Forty-Niners did was to pass regulations that Indians could not file gold claims. Indians could be hired by whites, and sometimes they were, but Indian rights were usually not observed. Miners would not allow Southern gentlemen to use their slaves to file claims and mine gold — miners would not allow slavery. The state of California was admitted into the Union as a Free State. The blacks were free to file their own claims. Mining camps made their own rules before the law arrived. They set up people's courts to settle disputes and preserve the peace.

Treaty rights of Spanish settlers were also violated in the Wild West. California kept the Spanish names of the major cities established along the Coast. It is an interesting fact that the Spanish law gave more legal rights to women than the law that we had inherited from England, Rome and earlier civilizations.

Spain established the first universities in Mexico and South America. They had lead-time over the New England universities — but they produced few scientific and technological achievements. They gave priority to pushing religion rather than education, in their learning institutions.

The Spanish Inquisition and the banishment of the Jews and Arab Moors had some part in the decline of Spain. Their prominent role in the upper echelons seems to have caused great resentment and distrust. Religious persecution drove out from Spanish society educated teachers, doctors, philosophers, lawyers, successful merchants and bureaucrats. Some of the Jews fled to the Eastern Mediterranean and some ended up in the Middle East as far as Yemen, Iraq, and Syria.

American imperialism did not to stop with the acquisition of the Western states through war. Later administrations would take Guam, Midway, Cuba, Puerto Rico, and the Philippine Islands in a war with Spain. Missionaries grabbed the Hawaiian Islands with the rationale that if we did not steal them, another great power might take possession of that Polynesian chain.

It is an often-repeated lie that the United States is not practicing imperialism today. We are currently practicing military imperialism with the goal of setting up puppet regimes all over the Middle East and into Asia, as well as in Latin America. Our forte is economic imperialism and dollar diplomacy; we enrich corrupt elites of other countries and indebt them in order to gain access to natural resources. If they refuse to collaborate, then we look for their rivals to put in power with an election or a coup. If our jackals fail, then we may resort to sending marines or armed intervention. We have been doing that in Latin America since the 1800s.

American bases have not left Greenland or Iceland since World War II. We have hundreds of foreign bases, from Germany, Japan and Korea to Qatar and Aruba. They were not established for our defense, they were established so we could dominate the oceans and the trade routes, and so that our business interests would have access to the world's resources.

The Navy goal is no longer to gain control of the world's waterways, the new navy doctrine is to use the world's oceans. This nation has close to eleven battle groups that can be sent anywhere in the world, and with air cover. No wonder other nations fear, rather than respect, our aggressive policies. Fear is the breeding ground for hate.

The reason you no longer see anti-American protestors in the world's streets is because they are in factories making weapons. Sovereign states may engage in an arms race to defend themselves against the "New World Order." New alliances are being studiously built by nations that see American invasions and attacks all around the world and wonder who is next.

Costa Rica is a curiosity. They had a revolution around 1948, dissolved their standing army, and put their funds in a police force, health, and education. It is the only Central American country to escape the violent wars that ripped through Panama, Nicaragua, El Salvador, Honduras, and Guatemala. Unfortunately, our intelligence agencies are involved in those crimes. But US history books have whitewashed the criminality carried out by American businesses in Latin America. The United Fruit Company is one of them.

The United States used its 'Monroe Doctrine' to exclude other colonial powers from getting access to Mexico and Central and South America. In the past, we intervened in other nations' political affairs because we wanted their resources from banan-as, coffee, copper, and lumber, etc. Now it's for drugs, miner-als, oil and gas. In turn, we want to sell them our manufactured goods. Our society was enriched. Mexico has many American banks in it; that could be a reason we loaned money to Mexico when they devalued their Peso.

Over forty thousand Mexicans have been killing each other. The government is fighting drug cartels that are rumored to be supported by federal agencies I the United States. Isn't that a civil war in North America already? Emigrants from Mexico come for jobs. Emigrants come from Central America to save their lives, and escape political instability. People vote with their feet. They come to the United States for better opportuni-ties — after we destroy their homelands.

CHAPTER 20: OUT OF COLLEGE AND INTO THE WORK FORCE

Juvenile delinquents taught me about crime. I worked for six months in a state institution after graduating from college. At night, I worked with three brain-damaged professional fighters in a state mental hospital during my sophomore year. I did not approve of boxing even with padded gloves. It saddened me that Joe Lewis ended up opening doors in a Mafia-owned casino in Los Vegas. At least the Mafia had some compassion for a brain-damaged fighter that had battered his opponents to the floor.

Then I worked several months for an international corporation in San Francisco. Whilst there I quickly learned that corporate criminals not only had college degrees, they also majored in law. I had majored in social studies.

I cannot call history a science when it is full of so many lies, omissions, and part truths, but sociology, anthropology, economics, criminology, psychology, social psychology, political studies, and history courses taught me about society. The only women I encountered in history courses were people like Catherine the Great, Queen Elizabeth, Queen Isabella, Catherine de Medici, and Dolly Madison. History books were about Man, or God. It was after I left college that women's studies, programs, and minorities came into being.

The family-owned corporation in San Francisco was a conglomerate. They built pipelines in the Middle East; they had built vessels during World War II; they had helped build the Boulder Dam during the not so 'Great' Depression; they owned their own tool company; they owned their own insurance company; their engineers had built bridges and nuclear plants; they had even got themselves on Sixty Minutes for their shenanigans for profit; and they padded their profits by burying truckloads of their brand new tools in pits in the middle of the night.

The first fascinating thing I learned about this corporation was this: All five vice presidents had gone to Stanford University; all were males; all had been fraternity brothers; and all had law degrees no matter what branch of the company they managed. This company had carpets on the executive floors that your feet sank into. They had original impressionist paintings on the walls and, reportedly, Picasso paintings in the bathroom. Those paintings were investments. They replaced the office furniture on the top floor every year. The first secretary I talked to had a master's degree from the University of Chicago. They had well-trained staff and were well-compensated for their skills. A Cornell PhD. was investing their funds in other companies on Wall Street. The board chairman read the Wall Street Journal and Kiplinger letter. The executive met to discuss the Great Books.

Since I was an office boy, I opened up the mail and delivered it to every floor of the company. In doing so, I discovered that these lawyers really did know the law. Every time they circumvented the law, their mail had the word 'Confidential' written across the envelopes. I quickly learned that 'so-called' competing insurance companies, our largest, cooperated. They contributed money to finance an attorney to run for office in a Southwest state. As a legislator, he introduced a bill that required every contractor in the state to provide insurance for their employees. Market share was already divided up among the cooperating companies. State percentages were modeled on existing national portions. This was not competition, it was collusion. These companies indirectly legislated profits by acquiring their own legislator to introduce laws that benefited the insurance industry.

When city and county workers were trying to get pay raises, the company in collaboration with other companies created a so-called "citizens group." They put together a war chest, rented an office, and campaigned to defeat the workers so they could keep their taxes low. False flagging of their interests was never an ethical problem for the company. They knew a year ahead of union leaders who the Justice Department was going to indict and imprison. Their intelligence networks were very good nationally and internationally.

I talked to their "glad hander" who met Arab sheikhs and foreigners at the airport. He spoke seven languages, according to him. He wore an English tweed sports coat, and he showed me his expense account for one month. He had spent thirty seven thousand dollars on drinks, meals, and accommodation for the good will of guests. All tax deductible as a business expense.

The company had two members going to the White House as members of presidential cabinets (State Department and Defense Department). I bounced my car off the wall of The Berkeley Tunnel one morning with a blow-out. I was late for work and the Chairman of the Board did not get his Wall Street Journal, and mail, on time as a result. They canned me for that ostensible reason. I suspect they did not approve of me opening and reading their confidential memos. The office manager actually said that I did not have the right attitude. All five vice presidents were very egalitarian and friendly to me. My name was the same as a deputy district attorney's. So they all approached me at coffee break in the cafeteria at different times. I assume they thought I was a useful connection, in case they ever came to the attention of the district attorney. I read the memo from the chairman of the board of directors. He was also owner of that company. He advised each vice president how much each was to donate to the political campaigns of various politicians. I thought it was a clever way for lawyers to channel corporate funds into political campaigns. The vice presidents received ample Christmas bonuses. I assume that may have been one method for their re-imbursement. At the time, there were laws against corporate money being funneled into political campaigns. Years later, I noted that the family-owned engineering company also built nuclear reactors that later leaked radioactivity into waterways. Today, some of your taxpayer's money is going into their hands as they are rebuilding some facilities in Iraq that were destroyed in the war to replace Saddam Hussein.

The company left Iraq as too many civilian contractors had been killed. Americans do not even know how many Iraqi people were murdered during the Bush Wars, the President Clinton sanctions, and ever since. I would venture that it is close to two million people — dead. Over 800,000 people, mostly children, perished with the Clinton era sanctions. Madeleine Albright famously stated that she thought it was worth it. More humanitarian citizens have suggested she be taken to a mental hospital for observation.

Do not forget that over half of all Iraqis are under the age of eighteen. We now have about 1.1 billion people on the planet who fear and hate us, and with good reason. That is just the people living between Morocco and Indonesia. The figure does not include our former friends in Europe and in Britain.

Chapter 21: Drifting Toward Civil War In North America

Many of us were surprised when the Communists became discredited in their own country. They had another revolution, a sow one that did not take many lives.

The Soviet Union devolved into its fifteen republics and the empire abandoned centralized economic control. They now operate a mixed economy where free market principles allow private property and private businesses to develop, and their vital resources are no longer in the hands of a single state monopoly. Politically, they have regular elections and have expanded the concept of personal freedom. In the process of privatization, powerful individuals and small groups 'grabbed' ownership of some industries and hired bodyguards, and they went through a phase similar to our age of robber barons, but after the first twenty years the worst of that was brought under control. However, what is perhaps most interesting, they still have a national industrial policy that allows them to identify some priorities and to reduce unnecessary redundancy, being more efficient.

The former Soviet State had a monopoly of economic, political, military, and media control. Party bureaucrats, and dictators, had controlled every aspect of Soviet life — including their music, education, literature and arts. Yet, a Communist society had fragmented into ethnic Republics. This was unforeseen by the Western powers. The historical lesson here is that — even with the totalitarian social control — society can undergo massive change. Their populace decided that the power of the states was no longer legitimate, or worthy of their support.

The United States had very different social institutions, customs, and values, and now — a questionable political system. Suspicions of fraudulent elections in the last several presidential cycles do not instill confidence. We had alternating rulers with two major political parties — we did not have a single dominant political party — and both parties supported private property. The United States had a better civil rights record after the civil war, and slavery was abolished. England abolished slavery before we did; I was shocked to learn that Sweden was the last nation in Europe to abolish slavery, after 1900.

Our first "civil war" was when we overthrew British rule and became a small independent country. We managed to survive because the other European empires were gobbling up lands in Africa, Asia, the Middle East, Oceania, and Latin America. Those militaristic empires fought among themselves, and we were determined to go from sea to sea and dominate our southern neighbors who had also broken away from European civilizations. George Washington put down Shay's Rebellion and the Whiskey Rebellion with force.

The next "civil war" was when the Southern states broke away, and that caused massive loss of life and the destruction of Southern property. The industrial North smashed Southern aristocratic ambitions, and left a nation scarred for generations. The South called it the War Between the States. Their reading of the Constitution shows that they had a right to secede from the Union.

Contrary to most of our notions, the slavery issue was not the paramount reason for mass slaughter. Regionalism was: competition between industrial and agrarian interests, and tariff protection to help the growing industries in the North at the expense of the South, also had a part in creating social conflict. Immigration, opening up new lands, and ethnic differences, were probably contributing factors to a war between our industrial elite versus the landed aristocracy of the Southern plantations. The issue of where to draw a line between States' rights versus strong federal control divided the nation.

There were a few politicians who challenged others to duels, and one Southerner accepted a challenge — with cannons as his choice of weapon — across the Mississippi River. In the West, Samuel Clemens chose cow pies when an irate reader of one of his columns challenged him to a duel.

The West is a blot on our history. A hundred years after wiping out the native populations along the Eastern Seaboard, our ancestors started making their way westward and continued to apply the alien concept of land ownership as private property. They invaded and conquered Stone Age peoples, and they practiced genocide. Successive Congresses, and white settlers, broke most of treaties they signed. Poor immigrant Europeans were greedy for land and its mineral resources.

Proud as Americans are of the principle of "private property," the foundation of private property ownership is in killing and stealing. This misbehavior was against Christian dogma. Religious folks had complex rationalizations for their barbaric conduct toward the misnamed Native Americans. Some claimed that the primitive people had no souls, and that they were just animals anyway. Social progress was moving slowly, or perhaps in reverse.

One fourth grade history textbook in California mentioned the thousands of natives that died from the lack of immunity to diseases brought in by the new settlers. It also explained that the Indians "disappeared"; there was no mention that settlers, ranchers, and posses, had hunted and killed over 40,000 of the State's original inhabitants. A Stanford history researcher arrived at that figure from a newspaper account of those shameful days. Contrary to the impression of old Hollywood movies, it was the US Army who rescued the remnant of the Mattole River Indians when their white neighbors massacred a village at Squaw Creek. A small group attacked the village after Indians had killed a cow that became mired in a muddy creek bed. The leader hated Indians and probably wanted their land. Only a few men started the massacre, after most of the village males had gone down to the beach for shellfish. They killed the old men and young boys first, and then they killed the women and children.

This Indian massacre occurred In Humboldt County. When the killers ran out of bullets, they were stabbing the children that had fled into the brush. An Indian teenager was found after the Army had left. He was given to a widow near Honeydew. He was spared so he could work, cut wood, and do chores, but he kept running off and finally he too was killed. The army relocated the survivors at Covelo, in Northern California.

Early Humboldt residents were racially intolerant. The Chinese in Eureka had a Tong War and a stray bullet killed a prominent citizen near the Courthouse. The community threatened to lynch all the Chinese in the area, and subsequently drove them out of the County. They were forced to leave on a ship that was bound for San Francisco. Word of their arrival spurred the San Francisco authorities to meet the unwanted at the docks. The Chinese jumped overboard and swam to shore with whites chasing them down. Many fled into Chinatown, where they melded into the population. The Chinese lost all their businesses and property in Eureka and in the nearby communities.

Before the big Civil War there were conflicts in this nation by many groups who were intolerant of others. Mormons were persecuted in the East, and subsequently migrated to Utah. Range Wars were fought between cattlemen and sheepherders. A County War was waged in New Mexico that gave Billy the Kid his notoriety. In Nevada, the whites discovered that Paiute warriors were formidable enemies. The Apaches also fought white invasion well enough and were given larger reservations than the more peaceful Indians were. American history has numerous examples of social conflict. General Custer, and elements of the 7th Cavalry Regiment, were defeated by Crazy Horse and Sitting Bull. General Eddington committed genocide at Wounded Knee. In other incidents, the Army gave smallpox-infected blankets to Indians, and Generals Sherman and Sheridan disposed of other Native Americans in a series of wars, after the Civil War.

Given our violent history and current social tensions, and the apparent failure to learn the need to get along with each other, a new Civil War may be inescapable. This is more than States' rights versus Federalism.

There are factions that still espouse the faith of their grandfathers, restoring a state religion in order to try to create a sense of commonality would be dangerous as this society has many different religious groups that do not agree on each other's principles. Racial discrimination too has the potential of erupting into racial conflict. The increased disparity between our wealthiest and poorest could evolve into class warfare. The failure to provide fair elections could lead to a situation where bullets could replace ballots. Fraudulent elections, and money-sponsored candidates, risk social instability. The big lies of a complicit media can hide the problem for some time and public relations companies can still spread their myths, but more than half the population no longer believes that Congress and the State Houses represent them.

The neo-conservative agenda is in conflict with the values and traditions of most citizens, as Americans are not comfortable with the establishment of a corporate state. Corporations have succeeded in reducing the political powers of trade unions. Out of office, the neo-conservatives sought to reduce the power of government to regulate the private economy. Once in power, the neo-conservatives enacted laws to consolidate their power. FEMA and the Patriot Act are examples of contingency plans to enhance social control.

FEMA provides for the declaration of martial law in the event of a natural or social disaster. Martial law bypasses Congress. Under these provisions, if the government labels any citizens as "terrorists," the Bill of Rights in our Constitution no longer applies and becomes nothing but an antiquated parchment.

A few years ago, a book was published shoeing the results of a poll asking the American people about their attitudes toward one hundred forms of occupation. (What Do Americans really think?) It merely ranked people by those who had the most esteem, and on the very bottom those that had the least esteem. At the time of the poll, the following opinions were expressed: Paramedics and Firemen ranked number one and two in esteem, and elementary school teachers were ranked number four — higher than Supreme Court justices, college presidents, dentists, accountants, bankers, clerks, mechanics, college professors, TV executives, newspapermen, and many other occupations. Lawyers were placed in the lower 50%. Dentists were ranked higher than doctors — it is probable that HMOs contributed to their lower ranking. Lawyers and TV executives were not highly ranked in the esteem of the public. A recent poll showed that 45% of the populace no longer trusts the media!

Drug dealers and Mafia bosses were ranked last. Our citizenry despises members of the criminal class. Prostitutes were ranked above United States Congress-people in public esteem!

Another poll indicated that the majority of citizens believe the Federal government has been commandeered by "Special Interests." In other words, most people no longer believe that their Republic is operating as it was intentionally designed. If this is true, it means that the Democratic myth is eroding. Most members of society sense that they do not have any power, and major political institutions no longer represent their needs. Some feel that the Government is useless in addressing their social concerns. They often complain, but have not taken action as yet.

What led to our present state? The people want health, education, decent jobs, clean air, and water. The people want a Welfare State and not a Warfare State targeted against 'so-called' terrorists. Our successive governments have funded and trained the terrorists that we fight today. Some of these jihadists are former CIA assets. We used them for our own warfare needs and now we are using them against us.

There have been great strains on the United States, in the past, which could have led to a dis-United States — but did not. The not so 'Great' Depression, or economic collapse, had a far-reaching impact on politics. J. Edgar Hoover's secret files have provided historians with some volatile information about the American power elite families operating in 1933. The Stock Market crash in 1929 plunged us into bank failures, family bankruptcies, small business failures, the closure of factories, massive un-employment, and farmers lost their land. It caused economic stagnation and a political crisis. Radical movements on the right and left, formed in answer to the collapse of the privately owned economy. That business cycle resulted in starvation for some, and soup kitchens appeared in our cities. The Hoover administration lost the confidence of the American people and Franklin D. Roosevelt won the Democratic nomination.

"The American Liberty League" was formed by one hundred and fifty six wealthy industrial families who plotted to over-throw the government and establish a fascist state, a Corporate State, modeled after Hitler's Germany and Benito Mussolini's Italy. They sent two Wall Street lawyers to Europe to study those totalitarian social movements (Grayson M.P. Murphy and Gerald C. MacGuire). They approached our military leaders with a plan, but they would not go along with the plot.

General Darlington Smedley Butler and James Van Zandt — Commander of the VFW — were offered the funds and the task to overthrow the Republic. They both testified in closed Congressional hearings, and Congress covered up the plot to protect America's powerful industrial leaders who were sponsors of the conspiracy.

The plotters wanted to arm the Bonus Marchers in Washington, carry out a coup d'etat and kill Cordell Hull and Franklin D. Roosevelt.

These dynastic elite families had their spawn and minions change their organizational names

The original planners of fascism in the US failed in 1933, but the same dynastic power elite families changed the names of their organizations and trust funds. They passed their massive economic power on to their progeny with trust foundations, they had tax exemptions to perpetuate privilege, and they established right-wing think-tanks and wrapped themselves in the American flag. The children, and grandchildren, succeeded where their ancestors failed. They founded and funded more than a hundred right-wing organizations and many that appear to be Left as well, so they can dominate both sides of any debate.

No wonder the Supreme Court is so corporate friendly. Our largest corporations are the economic arms of the dynastic power elite families. No wonder 'the best above the rest' have created strong control over our institutions to protect their property rights. No wonder human rights for decent jobs, clean air, food, and water, are of such little concern to the government. Your health is not a primary concern of the few who make decisions affecting the safety of the many. The elite have eroded the "New Deal" programs of the Roosevelt era, and have diminished the Welfare State. Both major parties allowed the creation of the military industrial complex that has now given us the Warfare State. We are now have pre-emptive wars and tortured prisoners.

Franklin Roosevelt called these families economic royalists in the 1930s. Roosevelt and the liberal Democrats saved capitalism from its worst abuse of common citizens, and he did it by regulating the economy and putting checks on the power of the elite by allowing the creation of labor unions. He created Social Security, which lifted millions of seniors out of poverty, and that enabled young families to raise their children without the burden of the failing health of their aged parents.

The social issues that divide us today cannot be separated from the past. It is a question of values that has guided this nation ever since its inception, but in the past 20 years, conflicting values have been growing between the populace and the regime.

There will be social conflict in our future, in spite of the civilian detainee camps created to contain future popular dissent. The militarization of the police (including swat teams), and the takeover of National Guard units by Federal control ('in case of a national emergency'), are consolidation moves to bypass Congress. Should any popular resistance crop up, FEMA stands ready. FEMA id a coup plan that was not originally funded by Congress; providing aide in case of natural disasters was a cover. Their response to Katrina was in fact a rehearsal for their own benefit; obviously, they did not focus on helping those who were devastated by the hurricane.

The Liberal Democrats avoided a revolution in the 1930s, and with a glance over their shoulders ta the basic social security provisions provided in the Soviet Union, they established some humane programs in the US while seeking to avoid the heavy-handed regimentation that Communism is known for.

They were gradualist reformers. Who wanted civil war?

The Civil War in the 1860s — Americans killing Americans — was our greatest social disaster. It took the Southern generations to recover from that conflict. The South remained poor, while the wealth of the industrial North created powerful economic "robber barons" and thriving cities.

However, the first Corporate Welfare program, placing the interest of big money above those of the populace, came at around this time when Congress gave lands to build the railroads. That united the commerce of this growing nation. The Harrimans (Robber Barons), Vanderbilts, Huntingtons, Stanfords, and others, took the government land subsidies to build railroads, and then they used monopoly power to impoverish farmers in the Midwest and West. They used cheap non-union labor to create their vast fortunes and then many translated their economic power into political power.

The mechanization of agriculture increased productivity; however, the benefits never trickled down to farm workers. They were not allowed the power of collective bargaining for decades. The civil rights activist Cesar Chavez was the first to aid farm workers to form successful unions. Many foreigners came to America because we were enjoying a boom and there were many opportunities. Food was plentiful. The benefits of the Wagner Act aided factory workers in securing safety laws, pensions, annual vacations, negotiated medical care, grievance procedures, and wages, beyond subsistence.

Nationally, we needed to have big government curb the abuses of big corporations. Teddy Roosevelt — a Republican — tried to check the power of the elite with progressive laws. (Didn't he get shot?) Few, in past ages, foresaw corporations taking over the government from the people. It was a gradual process and few took notice. Evolutionary stealth politics was successful. The masses were propagandized to resist the evils of 'creeping socialism' and were sandbagged by an elite group with creeping capitalism. The irony is that this society developed with a mixed economy having socialism and capitalism in its basic institutions.

In the Thirties, Liberals used graduated income tax to sponsor programs that benefited all citizens. They created Big Government to solve big problems. The government borrowed money for employment programs to enliven a prostrate economy. The WPA and the CCC were created to provide jobs for hungry people that were destitute. General Patton managed the CCC, and thousands of carpenters, masons, electricians, and heavy equipment workers were created. Interestingly enough, they came in handy during the World War II.

The Welfare State was created to help small business, and destitute farmers, who were being pushed off the land by low prices for their goods. Keynesian economics and government spending programs were used in the recovery from the Depression. The graduated income tax was used to fund needed social programs. World War II spending finally brought on a full economic recovery, and the spoils of war kept the United States flush for a few decades. Women and minorities left home, and the South, to work in shipyards and war industries. The GI Bill, which came into effect after the War, gave us the most educated labor force in the history of the World. We had economic growth, and almost no competition until Germany and Japan were rebuilt. We created a middle class with education and a people friendly government. Civil rights, and women's rights, were increased, but not without protest and struggle.

Conservatives resisted social programs as they wanted to conserve their own power, and many of them were social Darwinists who extolled competition. They forgot the crucial role cooperation plays in a society. Around a hundred and five automobile companies had been reduced to less than five, and that was accepted as normal and desirable. We developed a car economy that relied on fuel and that led to aggressive foreign policies and wars. Competition seemed to make some Americans more equal than the general population: one percent of the population owned forty percent of the nation's wealth. Besides that, some controlled workers' pension plans.

The wealthiest hated Roosevelt and called him a Communist for his programs; they attacked all social programs through the press and radio, which were owned by private interests. For decades, the media has programmed the populace to fear and hate Communists and Socialists, and now, in a knee-jerk way, they persist in tarring Russia with the same hate-filled rhetoric where the truth is ignored and facts are made up. The upholders of the privately-owned economy fear social property, public lands, or economic enterprises that are owned by a government in the public's name. The elite families are against big government unless they can control it through their minions, and then they support the "Super Power" myth, nationalism, and militarism.

In the meantime, the schools teach millions that we are a Democracy and that votes count. The values of the people are in conflict with the goals of the few who want to privatize government. Two recent fraudulent elections indicate that fair voting no longer counts. That is one reason the majority of eligible voters no longer even try to express their desires. Big money, and the media, has filtered out populist candidates in both major parties in the primaries. Politicians who want to represent society fully are not funded because they do not get financial support, and the privately owned media ignores their issues.

Anti-Communism was the cornerstone of American foreign policy ever since the Bolshevik Revolution. Our elite were frightened the workers and peasants would seize factories, and land, and declare them as social property. Private property holders are always fearful of the means of production, distribution, and exchange, being controlled by a state. Those who want a corporate state fear Democratic states. The United States have supported un-democratic states abroad, even though they preach democracy here. The main criterion has been — will the economic policies give us access to the world's natural resources? The State Department, and the CIA, have overthrown governments and have assassinated foreign leaders in the name of business interests, and that is why we are unpopular abroad. Other nations fear the military power of the United States.

The dynastic power elite sponsored candidates to our Congress and State Houses to protect their privileges and current social power. Public Relations companies and lobbyists are handmaidens of special interests. The majority of persons on Welfare in this country are children who cannot vote. Basically, the current government does not represent the majority of people living in this country. Had the Conservatives supported a workable national health plan, we would all be better off and government would have a better name. Instead, today, they are using private companies and contractors to perform duties that are meant to be done by our military. They were always interested in profit margins, and failed to see that the government was formed for service and not to enrich the few.

The far right-wing thought that democrats went too far in giving workers the rights to bargain collectively. Their short-sighted policies — created to weaken and wreck the unions — will have this unforeseen result. Someday, they will not face union organizers but revolutionaries. How can you bargain with revolutionaries that are not interested in talking or bargaining? If we have a revolution, the hunting of the elite, and their families, will occur.

The New Deal reforms, and government oversight of the economy, avoided a civil war over the Depression crisis. Yet the de-regulation of business, by elected government officials, will lead to economic and political crisis that may lead to new Civil War.

When lobbyism first appeared in our State Houses and in Washington, it was not originally seen as a threat to our democratic institutions. Television, and campaign financing, became powerful influences on elections. The super majority rules in political bodies and seniority rules have always assured slow social change. It became more difficult for legislative bodies to address the problems of society. Too few of the poor, or middle class, people could afford to run for office. We ended up with most of our senators being millionaires. They are remote from their poorer constituents and fail to recognize the significance of citizens eating out of garbage cans. Billionaires indirectly rule this country, though they deny the fact.

Black teenagers   have about a 35% unemployment rate in our major cities, and there is unhealthy air in our cities and polluted water across the United States. Neither the neo-conservatives of the so-called Democratic Party that followed, with Barack Obama, did enough to protect the society from unemployment, nor implement social programs to reduce crime.

Both parties' politicians support a massive military spending program while letting roads, bridges, and schools fall into disrepair. They failed to modernize or integrate the transportation systems. Just try to get to our major airports. In Frankfurt, Germany, like most of Europe, the airport, bus services, and superior rail systems all converge into a convenient hub. In China and

Russia, major nationwide high-speed rail networks and super-highways are being built at breakneck speeds. Yet we think we can claim to be the 'Sole Superpower.' We can't even keep the bridges from falling.

This nation opted for a car-conomy that kills over fifty thousand people a year. The oil and gas companies and the auto industry have prevented the development of a more rational transportation system and a plan for sensible growth. Firestone, General Motors, and Standard Oil, all made massive profits on Los Angeles freeways. The sensible, less polluting, electric rail system was foolishly discarded. Today, buses running on natural gas would be better than gridlock. Cities could have been better planned in some regions.

Congress needs reform if it is ever to address social needs. Seniority rules make some members more equal than others. A two-thirds majority rule (super majority) means our legislative bodies have minority rule, and minority rules are basically undemocratic and less adaptable to social change.

In the meantime, we live in overcrowded cities with inadequate housing for millions of our families. The white flight from the cities deprived our inner cities of taxes, and our cities deteriorated.

If tax burdens were lessened, rather than increased on improved property, there may have been less slums.

This society was always been unbalanced in regards to funding the education of our young. At one time, in California, a certain school district was paying $770 a year in order to educate an elementary school student — in Marin County, they invested over $5,500 per elementary student. Wealthy districts provided more programs, and their test scores reflected that some districts were underfunded. This problem of inequitable education funding was a national problem, but it never became a national concern with a national commitment to finding and funding a solution.

While Rhode Island expended over $5,000 per pupil, Alabama was expending less than $400 on their future citizens. On the other hand, states like Minnesota prepared their youth for the future, while some states, with a fundamentalist religious fervor, undermined science instruction and biology programs and regarded them with superstition. Science studies the natural world, while fundamentalist religions deal with the supernatural world. Currently, intelligent design advocates want to contaminate science classes with religion. Our founding Fathers separated Church from State to avoid the religious wars which plagued our European ancestors. Even the different Christian Churches are not in agreement, and unless we intend to limit the freedom of religious conviction, there will always be plenty who do not accept the basic precepts of Christianity either.

Religion has no place in the schools. People can set up other institutions for that, if they so wish. Ancient peoples worshipped numerous gods and goddesses, as they marveled at nature. Science can only study the natural world and universe — as yet, it has been unsuccessful in understanding supernatural phenomena. Religion relies on faith, while science relies on physical evidence to understand nature.

Some school districts concentrated on reading, writing, and arithmetic and gave less support to art, music, languages, and science. To be effective, languages should start being taught in kindergarten and first grade, not later, in high school, when language instruction is already less effective. Swiss children learn four or five languages by introducing language skills at an earlier age. Schoolchildren enjoy art and music, and some could even like science if the scientific method was taught properly and they were not put in a position where they became overwhelmed with irrelevant facts. Poor textbooks create anti-intellectual students and condition them for failure. The super-rich attack public education, because they have their children in private schools.

Let us examine another aspect of life. This subject is our reformed tax structure. In 1968, Ferdinand Lundberg wrote about our 'rich' and 'super-rich'. He used Internal Revenue Service data in his book. It revealed that 112 millionaires did not pay a dime of Federal taxes, because there were loopholes in the tax laws. (One year, Gulf Oil in California was tax free, but California citizens did not have that luxury.) The Midwest had two billionaires doing banking offshore that paid no Federal taxes — they owned cruise lines. Millions of Americans are being taken for a ride without knowing it, and it is not a ride on a cruise ship!

It got far worse: In 2011, over 4,000 millionaires paid no federal income tax, and over 400,000 tax filers with incomes over $100,000 paid no federal income tax.

Andrew Mellon, a former Secretary of the Treasury, was the first to coin the phrase "Tax reform" regarding reducing taxes on the rich. Dan Rostkenkowski — a Democrat — and numerous others, "reformed" the tax codes at least four times during the Reagan Presidencies. A decade later, a change came upon our society. The super-rich, or their tax accountants and lawyers, read the book. They benefited from reduced taxes with new loopholes, and maybe some closed doors to wealth. Dan Rostenkowski went to jail for some crimes, and the nation had to shift the tax burden to the non-privileged.

It took over 200 years to get fourteen billionaires in this country. After the Reagan era, we suddenly had over forty billionaires, as the tax burden was shifted to the middle class and poor.

It is estimated that there are six million other people now avoiding Federal Income Tax. Surely, that can be interpreted as passive resistance if not outright tax rebellion! We have an inequitable tax structure and it will eventually lead to revolution. People's courts will not be collecting back taxes as history reveals that revolutions occur when the society has an unfair tax system.

This nation could have had a revolution when a cabal that included members of both major political parties assassinated John F. Kennedy. It did not, because the FBI concealed the crimes of the CIA, and also those of prominent dynastic elite families. The cover-up was successful and government records were sealed for 75 years to avoid prosecution of the guilty — and the explosion of the people.

The plotters gained the cooperation of law enforcement agencies with the cover of "possible foreign involvement." The threat of nuclear war, and the need to protect national secrets, was used to gain cooperation of some investigators who were ordinarily law-abiding people. Over seventy witnesses were killed and many disinformation books were published for limited hang out of portions of the truth.

Jack Kennedy had ordered the partial withdrawal of troops and advisors in South Vietnam on a Thursday, and by Friday, he had been assassinated. The following Monday, Lyndon Johnson was the new President, and he cancelled the troop withdrawal order and started the escalation of the war. This satisfied the "Military Industrial complex." Our most powerful elite received massive profits, and at the same time conditioned the public to fear and hate Communists. The demise of three hundred American soldiers and airmen per week eventually distracted the populace from thinking about the gunshots at Dealey Plaza.

When Martin Luther King Jr. was assassinated, the nation's minorities were aroused to arson and rebellion. Portions of American cities burned. Poverty and discrimination were at the root of a great deal of social discontent. The conclusion of a governmental commission was ignored by the power structure. Another mini civil war.

Bobby Kennedy was killed the night he won the California primary. He was in favor of getting our men and women out of Vietnam's civil war. He and Jack had contemplated breaking the CIA into little pieces after the failed "Bay of Pigs" invasion of Cuba. They fired Allen Dulles, the director of the CIA. But it was the Kennedys who got themselves dead.

The political struggle continues within our own society, under ever new guises. Where are the peace candidates? In 2016, Hillary made it clear she wanted war NOW, and because Trump said we'd better wait until we get those fighter jets working, he risks being overthrown. That's a new war they're talking about, before we find our way out of Iraq, Afghanistan, Libya and Syria.

A look at domestic policy: Some Congressmen have actually argued against raising the minimum wage for workers. They claimed it would ruin the economy and affect teenagers who might lose their jobs. Meanwhile, there are New York stockbrokers being paid a billion dollars. How could our economic system reward a few people who move numbers around with such economic power? They don't produce anything.

The disparity of incomes between our rich and poor does not seem just or supportable. Why are decent wages damaging to the character of the poor, and a sign of success gained by the affluent?

Social Darwinists see welfare programs as bad for the needy, while outlandish financial gain is acceptable by the greedy. There is something drastically wrong when the productivity of workers goes up while their standard of living goes down. Blaming the unseen hands of the market is a social myth. Men in boardrooms make the decisions as to how much they pay their workers for the production of goods and services. Breaking up unions and exporting jobs overseas reduces our work force to David Ricardo's iron law of wages, and puts too much power into the hands of owners and managers.

American executives are paid much higher than Japanese executives. It takes the total earnings of a husband and wife, with second jobs, for struggling American families to keep a roof over their heads these days. Advertising, and easy credit, has saddled many families with massive debt. If they get sick or are laid off, they enter the bankrupt class

Successive governments have practically destroyed labor unions. That leaves the company shareholders as the only ones with any power at all, the only ones whose needs are addressed. The workers are squeezed, then kicked out.

Make no mistake about the possibility of a revolution. A revolution is when the bottom portion of society destroys the top. Many people dislike privilege in this country. They want economic opportunities for themselves and educational opportunities for their children. People do not like the health insurance programs that are privately owned and operated. HMOs are very unpopular.

For that matter, 50% of workers do not like their bosses. Many people resent the fact that corporation money went into the political campaigns of sponsored candidates. This happened in spite of "laws" put in place to prevent such economic power being translated into political influence.

In a revolution, lobbyists and public relations minions would be fleeing the country to save their lives. Mexico would be complaining about the sudden influx of gringos. Powerful dynastic families would be attacked by mobs taking revenge for what their grandfathers did to the republic. The elite have their own security forces and bodyguards; we may find out how well their gated communities, and vast estates, protect them from the "have-nots."

In Cambodia, the revolutionaries were agrarian peasants; they killed people who had eyeglasses because that marked them as city-people and people with money. They wiped out more than the government; they killed journalists, teachers, judges, and practically everyone who was literate. They adopted our former Vietnam strategy, "kill them all, and let God sort them out." That is what happens when people cannot differentiate their friends from their enemies.

Millions of innocent people get killed in revolutions. Revolutions are social disasters that occur when leaders mis-calculate what effect their policies have on the population. The dynastic power elite use polling methods to take the 'temperature' of society; they gear their political campaigns to the perceived mood of those that vote; and they give lip service to some social concerns, but usually have a hidden agenda. They say what the people want to hear, but that does not mean they follow through.

They use language very effectively to gain support and slander their opponents. Unfortunately, many citizens are susceptible to repeated lies. They divide the population with side issues and confuse the voters, distract the voters, and bombard them with patriotic symbols that already have the support of the majority. Ownership of mainstream media also has an impact on the bamboozled and the gullible.

The only good news is that most citizens no longer believe, or trust, mainstream media.

The dynastic power elite families would at first try to suppress the revolt with the military, CIA, Defense Department, and death squads. Many of our military are already leery of "spooks." While the military would ordinarily not be inclined to kill the citizens they are dedicated to protect, police and others are going to target practice to learn to shoot at pregnant women, children, and the elderly. This is to remove their natural inhibitions. Not a good sign.

The current President, like the others before him, cannot draft his own policies. In Trump's case, the situation is even more starkly evident. The right-wing think-tanks founded and funded by dynastic elite families, and Israeli apologists, can promote or block major policy initiatives. They control most of this nation's economy.

The separation of powers in the US is a blessing and a liability. Under George W. Bush it seemed the office of the President had too much power and that Congress failed to check the influence of the executive branch. It was thought that a total overhaul of Congress might be needed. Such an overhaul would include rejecting the seniority system, and perhaps abandoning the system of super majority voting would restore actual representation. Congress should look like the American people and not have so many of them as millionaires. The Senate is overrepresented by the affluent and their policies show it. Some of them have already declared class warfare on the American people. Congress surrendered their power to make war, which was a crucial misstep. Those wars may eventually come home with our disenchanted troops.

At the same time, to have judges around the country refusing to obey presidential orders directly undermines the careful balancing act that has kept the United States functioning throughout our history. When former presidents open offices to engineer the overthrow of a sitting president, that looks like treason. The president must be allowed to set policy and take responsibility for his own successes or failures. If a president proves to be incapable, we have procedures and provisions for dealing with it. But the legitimate president has to be allowed to do his job.

Another look at corporations and how they affected political parties: Some corporations have taken funds and have sponsored candidates to promote special interest legislation. Those expenses have been written off as business expenses on tax returns, and are in direct violation of laws in some States. It is done artfully with the connivance of lawyers and legislated loopholes. It also undermines respect for the law and the legal profession. Contrary to what some believe, some of the special interest legislators are not sent to Office to make laws; instead, they are often funded to block legislation by reformers. Our existing laws have given special privileges not available to common citizens and this is resented by millions of citizens. When the economic or political system has a severe crisis that citizen resentment may result in a drastic modification of existing institutions. The right-wing wants to de-power union money in politics. This overlooks stockholders political affinities when corporate money is siphoned off for political influence. Looking at Unions as being conspiracies, and overlooking malfeasance by corporations, is something than aggravates working people.

Lawyers are not popular in America because they are part of the unjust social system, yet they are an essential part of a complex society. The judicial system was organized to settle disputes and uphold the laws, but the population has seen the poor executed for murder, and the rich receive lighter sentences and even acquittal or hospitalization.

Millions of eligible voters no longer bother to vote — a glaring example of disenchantment. Many are not willing to affiliate with either the Democrats or Republicans. Questions of election fraud and rigged voting machines have not restored the confidence.

When William Jennings Bryan ran for the Presidency it frightened two of our wealthiest citizens. G.P. Morgan met with John D. Rockefeller — both had been competitors. Morgan had supported Edison and the invention of his electric lights. John D. Rockefeller was an oil baron whose fortune was founded on kerosene lighting. Both men agreed to fund the presidency of William McKinley.

When a person commits a crime, it is an act of defiance against existing law. It is an individual rebellion against the rules of the society. We do not rehabilitate criminals in the US, instead we punish them by incarceration. Our incarceration rate indicates that we do not have a stable society. This is another symptom of social unrest.

The role of the police is changing in America. Rather than being seen as public servants protecting law and order, they are known for breaking into homes in the dark of night, armed to the hilt and shooting on sight. No matter whether they go the right home or not. On the highway, if they stop you for going too fast — or too slow — they can search your vehicle and confiscate anything they deem "suspicious." Without charging you with any crime. Now, Americans fear the police rather than respecting them;

The nation should have a total employment policy and government jobs should be available when the private economy lays workers off. Agricultural workers should have been subsidized as much as big corporate farmers. Just four major corporations control most of our food production. Monopolies never favor a society.

In America, 25% of prisoners are mentally ill and they do not belong in prisons in the first place. Many were damaged by alcohol and drugs and should have been placed in a secure hospital setting with treatment programs.

Those who believe in capital punishment should be the first to experience it firsthand. Europeans abandoned capital punishment. It would be desirable to outlaw capital punishment from a human rights point of view. In hospitals and clinics, medication for the mentally ill should be compulsory and administered by qualified doctors and nurses.

The owners of great industries must be subject to government regulation to protect workers, consumers, and investors. Unregulated capitalism will lead to revolution and social distress. Governmental regulation is the only recourse that can keep individualism from trampling the rights of the majority of people.

The US government has allowed people to be tossed out into the streets — homeless. It is time for the people to toss the status quo out of office. Most of the homeless have serious mental, and health, issues that are not being addressed by society. There is nothing wrong with a Welfare State. The purpose of government was to promote the General Welfare, not create economic and political privilege for the greedy elite.

We now have a Warfare State with excessive amounts of tax dollars paying for armaments. We have neglected to carry out the health, education, and housing programs needed to take care of our own population.

This nation has too many people without an adequate health plan. This is unacceptable in a nation as wealthy as the United States. The government should compete with the private insurance companies and put them out of business. The nation's health is a national security issue. The Great Depression weakened our men and boys so much, over the period of a decade, that 40% of them could not pass an Army physical when they enlisted or were drafted to fight World War II. The average soldier gained over twenty pounds in training!

Regarding American corporations, the economic engines of our elite are companies like Lockheed, General Dynamics, FMC (Farm Machinery Corporation), and Bechtel Industries, just to name a few. They all produce equipment that helps us to fight our wars. All these corporations have had scandals, which have involved cheating the government and the taxpayers. To compound the outrage, the privately owned media castigates the government for wasting taxpayer money! The Federal government is attacked in print and the airwaves, while big corporations get away with breaking laws, violating business ethics, and not fulfilling contracts without over-charges.

Instead of arresting and seizing crooked companies, the government fines them and then continues to do business with criminal defense contractors!

Criminal businessmen tarnish the reputations of honest companies. Only government oversight, and regulation, can correct white-collar crime. *Laissez-faire* capitalism is a recipe for social disaster.

Seized, criminal companies should be put into receivership of the courts, and honest executives should replace those under indictment or convicted of fraud. Investors and workers need greater protection.

The real owners of America have a problem with the business cycle. When goods are over produced, or when the population is too poor to buy what is produced, growth stops and millions are put out of work as business fails. The ensuing panic, Depression, Recession, economic re-adjustment, slow down, and/or stagnation cannot be hidden with euphemisms. Bankrupt banks, failed companies, massive unemployment, and resultant poverty cannot be ignored, and they bring social instability.

The usual solution of massive military spending is a dangerous remedy for a domestic economic problem. Invading other weak countries to distract the populace is not a suitable solution to over speculation and falling markets. Besides, stealing another nation's resources creates enemies even among our allies.

All wars are planned, and are avoidable with sane diplomacy and compromise. Societies that arm themselves are preparing for wars. Our current Defense Department operates as an Offense Department. Many societies view us as world conquerors, as we have our battle fleets in every ocean in the world.

Instead of starting conflicts with foreign nations, this society has serious domestic problems that have been ignored by our elite. If one thinks that national debt is a problem, consider that 80% of this nation's debt is corporate debt, consumer debt for mortgages and car loans, and farm debt. Now that the future generations are in debt to the private banks, this compounds the risk for this nation's future. If the housing and stock market bubble bursts, there will not be enough funds when people go to their banks. They will find that their funds were invested somewhere else and disappeared overnight.

Capitalism, or the so-called free enterprise system, works very well for 1% of this nation, which owns 40% of the wealth. The stock market is the essence of our privately-owned economy even though workers and others have pension funds invested in it. When it crashes, there will be a social crisis that will become a political crisis, and possibly violent conflict.

Every social system is designed to meet human needs. When institutions fail, they are modified by reform or revolution. Gradualism disappears in national emergencies. America does not prepare and/or plan for future crises, yet Americans respond well when they have to address national issues. Our citizens are way ahead of Congress in recognizing the vital importance of their physical environment. For it is the citizens who are breathing the polluted air and drinking the bad water. It is their children in the major cities suffering lung damage.

The healthy portion of our economy was designed to satisfy our basic human needs. We cannot survive without good food, clean air and water, adequate temperature regulation, freedom from physical trauma, proper elimination of waste products, and sex to replace the life that is lost to aging, illness, accident, murder, and war. We have an unplanned economy, meaning that private unknown parties decide our economic fate. The unseen hand of the market is within the corporate boards appointed by elite dynastic families who are blind to their own shortcomings.

Those families are victims of their own propaganda, whose ideologies are not based on democracy or the good of society overall.

Populist candidates are supposed to be eliminated in the primary elections. If one slips through, as perhaps Trump can be considered, he is neutralized before he is even worn in. The media ignores citizen's candidates and they do not get massive campaign funds to run for office. (Trump, whether he is a positive presence or negative, actually funded himself.)

Big government was created to counter balance the power of big business. The "New deal," and "Fair Deal," attempts to counter the worst abuses of the wealthy and the powerful. Deregulation, however, and business capturing of the government, are leading toward social catastrophe.

Speaking of social catastrophe, only 25% of families are in traditional marital relationships, and with children? Industrialism started stressing traditional families as soon as the population was leaving the farms and moving to the urban areas and factories.

Most Americans do not realize that the "corporate welfare" subsidies for the rich far exceed the government aid to the poor. Oil depletions allowances, tax loopholes for industries, outright subsidization of land to railroads, government funding of NASA, and medical research, have benefited the technological and drug companies. They have been feeding out of the taxpayer's trough for generations. The privately owned propaganda agencies, have blinded the populace to believe otherwise.

There is a basic conflict developing between corporate institutions and people. This nation has had many historical crises that we have survived without the onslaught of civil war, but we are approaching an age when citizens witness corporate crime and governmental corruption, and they are losing their patience. Government lies about the recent wars have led some to question the legitimacy of the government.

The dynastic power elite families apparently do not know that they cannot survive if they waste citizens' lives, submerge future generations in debt and ignore the needs of society. They have successfully hidden their manipulations of political life in the past, so that until now people still believed that we are a democracy and that the republic still exists. But the last few regimes damaged the credibility of the Oval Office in the eyes of the public. Government lies have consequences.

Social change, and peace, can only come when we tire of death. During the World War II, many American soldiers were unable to bring themselves to shoot their fellow men, even those designated as "the enemy," even when under fire themselves in combat. An aversion to killing inhibited them, out of respect for human life. But since then, for decades, our movies, TV programs, cartoons and comic books have exposed young children and teenagers to endless scenes of killing. The content of media and entertainment has programmed our society to accept violence. The devaluation of human life is fitting for a civilization that has doomed itself.

Accommodation, compromise, diplomacy, conflict resolution skills, and cooperation, have not been properly valued as the essential strategies they are; survival depends on this, not on conquest by force. If our soldiers now come home from foreign wars with these perceptions further distorted, the young may decapitate the top levels of society without compassion or remorse. If our elite have programmed our young to accept Thomas Hobbes' view — that life is nasty, brutish, and short, and only strong rulers can survive — they have then created a self-fulfilling prophecy. Those who most favor capital punishment will experience it; and those who make Draconian laws for others will suffer for their own punitive creativity — punitive societies create their own pain. But cruel societies are eventually overthrown.

Our current wars may be expanded overseas, and eventually they will be coming home instead of our troops. It would have been better if we had recalled the military and returned them to safety, and a declared peace. Our psychopathic leaders, and lemmings, are currently running for the cliffs.

Historians have a difficult time pointing to the events that signal a change in the direction of a society. Some may point to the death of the Liberal President Franklin D. Roosevelt, and others may point to the proxy war against Communism — when

North Korea attacked our puppet regime in South Korea. Some may say the Taft Hartley Act started eroding the social power of the Workers Union activity. Some may even pose that TV allowed "special interests" to control the information citizens relied on to make choices. Some may point out that peak oil caused the decline, as most of our elite had economic power by controlling our energy sources. The civilization was based on cheap oil, coal, and uranium, as sources of energy. No one stopped them when certain families created a monopolistic control of nature's energy to create vast fortunes that enabled them to sponsor their candidates and penetrate the government. Some could point to the Cold War itself as a sign of decline, or the making of nuclear bombs that killed civilians in total war.

Others will look at when we depleted the world's fisheries, cut 97% of the old growth redwood trees, ignored the signs of climate change, and polluted our own water and air. All of these events are related to an era when global resources were plundered without thinking of future generations. Yes, finite resources are a large part of our current wars. Yes, some companies think they can replace nation states because of their acquired power. All our wars are symptoms of predatory economics with the false notion that if everyone pursues their own interest, the social interests will be served. The big fight in our future will be between what is in the interest of society, opposed to what is in the interest of cabals that believe they can dominate the whole planet. Neo-conservatives are not new, nor are they likely to give the world social peace. Democracy cannot be spread by invasion or freedom given to any society. We have not solved the problems of industrialism, nor gained social justice. Our elite has been breaking the very laws that hold a society together. They are blinded victims of their own ideological right-wing propaganda. Nature is unforgiving. The society that lies eventually dies.

The political stability of this country has not been risked since the last Civil War that ended in 1864 — until recently. This is what the people in the United States and Canada will have to deal with in the future. The North American plan for unification with Mexico and Canada will be resisted in all three countries. Most citizens have never even heard about the intergenerational bankers' plot. Today it has the status of a "conspiracy theory." It was a plan to unify North America and issue a new currency called the "Amero."

This is a replica of the plan espoused by international elites who already created the European Union and introduced the "Euro," a program whose flaws are felt throughout Europe. The United Kingdom is pulling away, in a highly controversial move. They will be followed by other nations who find that "union" is not helping them. It just adds a stifling bureaucracy of un-elected administrators who tell each nation what they can and cannot do. If you never heard about the plan for the "Amero," it's because the elite, who own the media, did not think you were important enough to be informed of their plans.

Some conspiracy theorists believe nations are maneuvered into wars, and then the people are offered a solution to war by ceding their sovereignty to all-enveloping structures like the League of Nations, or United Nations, and then a final world government managed by elite bankers who print the money.

Trade agreements like NAFTA and GATT may be seen as experiments and initial steps. Recently, the US was pushing hard for adoption of the trans-national structure of TPP, but it was finally rejected for being far too aggressive in undermining national interests — putting all power in the hands of multi-national corporations, unelected, with no responsibility for the citizens of the world!

Now, suddenly, Forbes Magazine points out that "Commu-nist China" is leading the world in pushing for free trade. China is leading a push for a new Free Trade Area of Asia–Pacific, whose terms appear to be less menacing for now. Trade agreements should not annul protections for workers but extend such rights to countries that do not currently provide them. They should not risk further erosion of environmental laws.

It was these corporate interests, always happy to make a buck off wars, off exploitation of workers, off tearing up the en-vironment, that bankrupted our nation, our communities, and states. It is they, not the average citizen, who got us where we are today. And since it remains the actual persons on the ground who will live with the consequences, there is a possibility of an-other civil war on the horizon. Hopefully, I am mistaken.

Most citizens are peaceful, and have faith that our institutions are amenable to our will. Families do not even think about going to war with their own government. However, the people in power have thought about a possible civil war. That is why they have constructed and refurbished camps across the nation, and even in Alaska, for possible "civilian detainees." Lt Col. "Ollie" North devised a plan to bypass Congress in case of a national emergency with the cover of a "natural," or "social," disaster, to be defined by those whose interests it serves. This was called FEMA. Congress funded it when the Clinton administration came into power. Contracts for white railway cars, equipped with manacles, have been given to the usual suspects. All these preparations are contingency plans if the populace becomes irate about the rigged elections, economic bubbles that bring widespread ruin, and the destruction of our children's future

Some of the elite persuaded President Johnson to cut short the Vietnam conflict when the generals informed him that they did not have enough troops to quell Vietnam and the restless young people in the United States at the same time. Nixon took credit for avoiding a war at home by making peace promises as the war dragged on for several more years. Great profits were made by the arms industries during that conflict, which killed over a million Asians. But such profits are made by destroying, by wasting resources, not by investing and building. Excessive military spending will eventually wreck any country.

The elite are heavily buying real estate in escape locations like New Zealand. It's not only because of environmental fears, but fear of social explosions. If this nation got angry enough to start a civil war, impeachment would not even be an issue — only congress can impeach. I have not even discussed what impact disillusioned veterans will have on the society.

Unfortunately, every new presidential administration has to work with many of the same entrenched bureaucrats in Washington. The machine can only be run by experienced professionals, not by newcomers, nominees of those who are elected every four years.

Chapter 22: Summary: What Happened To The United States?

The people lost control of their society. A small cabal of our richest and most powerful dynastic families got control of our major institutions. They own the media monopolies and they control the messages we are bombarded with from early childhood to retirement and beyond. They control the cartoons, the textbooks, the entertainment we see and the news. They use these to perpetuate myths like the notion that the American people have power through elections and that we are still a republic.

However, half the eligible population no longer votes — even in important, presidential elections — as many have lost faith in the two major parties. About a third of the citizens now see themselves as 'independent'. Politicians are held in low regard as they have been working for clients and special interest groups. The promotion of the general welfare is no longer a serious issue. We are a warfare state.

A government that would regulate business or correct the worst abuses of economic power no longer stands in the way of laissez-faire capitalism. We no longer have self-corrective checks and balances to restrain the power of the few against the many bewildered citizens.

Our wars are not wars of 'liberation' but wars to overthrow governments that we can't buy. If Libya announces a plan to boost African economic cooperation, we see it as a rival to be smashed. If Iraq suggests it will stop selling oil for dollars, it has to be destroyed. If Syria wants some modicum of a right to self-determination, it has to be splintered like Yugoslavia. We claim to be eliminating tyranny abroad when the Patriot Act assaults our own Bill of Rights here.

We are losing the right to rational thought and are propagandized with a web of lies from powerful corporations. This government does not protect us; it threatens us in many ways. It has no regard for the very environment that sustains us. It risks devastating wars. It ignores the health and educational needs of millions of citizens. It makes bacteriological weapons that threaten humanity at large.

This society is under-informed, programmed, misled and bamboozled by the media. The un-organized populace has been duped by a group that owns public relations companies, hires trained lobbyists and has platoons of lawyers to enforce their rules.

Our wars are un-winnable and our debt-based economy is faltering. We are beginning the last stages of Empire. Other nations are holding economic summit conferences to figure out how to protect their own economies when ours collapses. The fallout, however, will be more than economic.

General Wesley Clark wrote a book entitled, *Don't Wait For The Next War*. That "Next War" idea causes me unease. On June 8, 2015, *The Wall Street Journal* noted that Islamic State had seized $27 billion of Iraq's military vehicles. The Iraqi army lost four of fourteen divisions when they fled during the Islamic State onslaught that began with the seizure in and around Mosul. The officers were the first to run. We have not finished our last war. America keeps breaking up nations that it cannot then bring back to any form of equilibrium. We are creating the equivalent of nuclear meltdowns, centers of destruction that cannot be neutralized. Yet Americans still do not have a peace movement. They are numb with "shock and awe" at what the Neo-Conservatives have done to us. Our media will not tell us that we have bankrupted the government with militarism.

Chapter 24: On Treachery

History books are a necessary part of studying human activity, but they lack the sounder foundation that can be found in anthropology, biology, psychology, sociology, economics, geography, and political science — or what is generally referred to as social science or social studies. Political science, like history, contains fictions and social mythology.

In order to get their people to kill other people, governments use propaganda, and it starts with how we are taught in school.

I was working as a night clerk at the Berkeley Y.M.C.A. in the late 1950s. A young man came down the stairs and wandered around the lobby aimlessly. I sat behind a desk reading a book and ignored him until he approached the desk. He said he could not sleep as he had been having a nightmare. He had been in the Air Force and was sent on a mission to bomb and strafe North Korean soldiers — who were traveling disguised as civilians, crowding the roads whilst trying to flee the battlefront. He was told that the enemy were wearing civilian garb. His unit bombed and strafed thousands of people near a bridge. Later he drove up to the area where the attack occurred. He discovered thousands of bodies, including the elderly, adult civilians, children, and babies; he did not see troops or guns. He could not sleep nor remove the memory of what he had done and seen.

Books on the Korean intervention made no mention of that incident. Newspaper accounts never mentioned that the Leader of North Korea had been a guerilla leader who resisted the Japanese occupation of his country. It did mention that Kim Il-sung was a communist and a Moscow-trained general. It did mention that American prisoners of war, captured by the North Korean army, had been found along a road with their hands wired behind their backs — shot. But how can we assess our 'enemies' if we ignore their need to defend their territory from attackers? Is that right?

Years later, I found that Ho-Chi Minh also worked against the Japanese as an agent for the American Office of Strategic Services. During World War II, Ho was provided with weapons and ammunitions so he could report on Japanese shipping along the coast of the former French Colony — then known as French Indochina. Ho was a nationalist. He was a medical student who tried to attend the Peace Treaty at the conclusion of World War I. He believed President Woodrow Wilson's lies about the self-determination of people to form their own government. He was not allowed to attend the conference to speak to the world power that carved up empires and created new nations with the stroke of their pens. French Communists sent him to Russia, and he became a communist who constructed a Declaration of Independence for Vietnam, modeled after the US Constitution. After the conclusion of World War II, the French returned to shell Hanoi, with cruisers, and killed 5,000 Vietnamese in an effort to regain her colony lost to the Japanese. Russia — our former ally against Germany, Italy, and Japan — became our enemy, again. Wanting France as an ally against this rival, we abandoned the nationalist figure of Ho Chi Minh.

We fought a war against Ho Chi Minh after he kicked the French imperialists out of his country. We called it the Vietnam War, even though war was never declared by Congress, and even though we ended up fighting in Laos and eventually bringing violence to Cambodia. Over a million Asians were killed. Maybe this was in part related to certain eugenics ideas.

Vietnam was a proxy war against Russia and China. It made our rich industrialists richer. Do most Americans know that we intervened again in Panama to rid the nation of Torrijoes and put

Manuel Noriega in charge? Later we turned against our CIA asset, invaded Panama and disposed of Manuel Noriega; we broke the Panama Canal treaty; and protected an American-sponsored regime that was running secret wars in Central America, engaging in arms smuggling and drug smuggling. Their purpose was to bypass the Boland Amendment, passed by Congress. William Colby, a Director of the CIA, had previously run drug operations through the secretive agency during the Vietnam War. He turned over the death squads, drug operations, and arms smuggling, to William Casey. Colby died under suspicious circumstances; his successor Casey died of cancer. Manuel Noriega, another CIA asset, was lucky to survive and serve a prison term in the United States.

By now, most Americans were programmed to hate and fear Saddam Hussein, but they know little of his story. Saddam Hussein was an assassin who shot his way to the top of the Arab Socialist Ba'ath party. He was a CIA asset whom we funded in a war against Iran.

French, German, and American, companies gave Saddam the weapons to kill the rebelling Kurds — all for profit, of course. The war with Iran killed over a million Iranian and Iraqi citizens. Maybe another part of a eugenics plot.

Why would we support Saddam? Easy — because the Iranian revolution kicked our puppet — the Shah — out of power and established an Islamic Republic.

British intelligence agencies have supported Islamic fundamentalist religious movements since the 1870s. That was one of their ways to prevent Arab nationalism or Nasserism. Great Britain was an empire that had colonies all over the planet; they did not lose that empire until they exhausted themselves in two World Wars. Empires are constructed and dismantled by mass violence. Advanced Western countries had no qualms about fomenting religious fervor that prevented Islamic societies from pursuing science and modern technology.

The Muslim world does not "hate our freedoms." That is one of the dumbest misleading slogans ever heard. Our "freedoms" are luxuries that no one cares about when their city is being blown up and the food supply has stopped. America did not help Afghanistan to rebuild their shattered infrastructure and there was no Marshall Plan to aid in rebuilding schools, clinics, water and sewage infrastructure, and local industry. The Taliban (religious students) came and drove other tribes north, and refused to make a "good" deal for the American oil companies to build a natural gas pipeline from a Soviet state through to Pakistan.

Al Qaeda reportedly blew up two US embassies in Africa. In this age of "false flag operations," third parties set off bombs to get others to fight. Who knows who did this?

Of course, most world citizens had the opportunity to see the videos of two planes flying into the World Trade Center buildings. Fourteen countries had warned America of a plot to hi-jack airliners and fly them into buildings. The Russians, Italians, Jordanians, and many other intelligence agencies warned of impending attacks. Mossad agents filmed the attack from a flat-bed truck. Police at first detained them, and later released them when they produced diplomatic passports.

You will not find this in the history books. David and Nelson Rockefeller built the Twin Towers. Building Seven, nearby, collapsed although it was not even hit by the planes. It housed the IRS, FEMA, and New York City's own security office, and other vital government agencies. Enron records were destroyed. That alone is enough to make one suspicious. The Swiss insured it and the owner said, "We had to bring the building down." Video pictures of the collapse suggest a controlled demolition as flashes of light and blown out glass were visible. No lives were lost in Building Seven. A French physicist, among others, pointed out that jet fuel does not burn hot enough to melt steel beams; no other building reinforced by steel has ever collapsed in a fire. The company belonging to Marvin Bush had access to the WTC buildings when custodial and security staff was sent home for a few nights. Of the 42,000 people working in the WTC Twin Towers, around 3,500 died there.

Some employees were told not to come to work on the day of the attack. There were unusual stock exchange activity on airline stock prior to the attack. One of the planes hitting the Towers had a pod under the nose of the plane not seen on commercial airliners. Video showed a flash of light coming out of the pod just prior to striking the building! Some witnesses said it did not appear to be an airliner because of windows and a lack of company insignia. Firefighters and police in the buildings felt an explosion in the basement, and they said, "Bombs were going off." One building had been attacked by a truck bomb years earlier; was it a test? Some of the men responsible in that operation were caught. They had been trained by Green Berets, not mentioned in earlier accounts. The same company that cleaned up the WTC attack cleaned up the Murrah Federal Building bombing in Oklahoma City. TV and video accounts initially stated that a bomb, or bombs, was found in the Murrah Building! That bombing too was attributed to Islamic radicals. When the WTC and Pentagon were attacked, our vaunted military had already stood down. Yet many Americans still cling to the idea that "we were attacked" by Muslim radicals because they hate us. Even if you accept that part, who hired them? That's the question.

The Project for the New American Century people — the neo-conservatives — have said that an attack like one that occurred at Pearl Harbor would be necessary to mobilize the populace for war. I suggest to you that these folks are not traditional Republicans.

Treachery is betraying a trust; it is the breaking of an alliance. Something that has a false appearance is treacherous. It is traitorous and treasonable. It is perfidious and a part of this nations black history. When a nation turns against an ally, that is treacherous. Breaking treaties is treacherous. The neo-conservative government broke the treaties and Geneva Conventions on the treatment of prisoners of war by torturing and murdering prisoners of war. That endangers all our military in future conflicts. The government is losing legitimacy in the eyes of the populace. I cannot conceive how this nation can regain its stature in the world without the trials of national leaders who broke our own, and international, laws.

We need to stop buying other nations and destroying them if they refuse to be bought. By trying to conquer the world, we are destroying large portions of the planet, as well as our youth. The people must regain control of the government. The purpose of government was — and is — to serve human needs; yet it is now funded and thus controlled businessmen.

CHAPTER 25: THE WAY IT IS TODAY

Public relations firms were created to protect the rich and socially powerful. They have no other purpose than to deceive the population of our society.

The media came under the control of the dynastic elite families when John D. Rockefeller was instructed, by banking interests, about the advantages of owning the press. That included magazines and books, as well as newspapers. Then a Hollywood movie studio was bought by an oil company. Prescott Bush was once a board chairman of CBS Radio. The du Pont influenced NBC, but even then the public was not alarmed.

When a poll showed that John D. Rockefeller was the most hated man in our society, the public relations industry was created to take the rough edges off that man. Some of the hatred was a result of his massacre of men, women, and children in a Colorado miners' strike.

Henry Ford and Andrew Carnegie also spilled citizen' blood when workers formed unions and struck the factories. They hired criminals to shoot protestors, but they also got the police and National Guard to come out and protect their property interests, and put down the workers.

Cabals have been killing our presidents and presidential candidates for over 150 years. Every killing was a 'conspiracy' in the sense that more than one person had to know about it, if not participate in setting it up. There were three CIA people in the room when Bobby Kennedy was shot. The airplane crashes that killed Senator Heinz, Governor Carnahan, Senator Wellstone, Senator Ted Kennedy, Treasury Secretary Brown, Torrijoes, and Pervez Mushariff's predecessor could not all have been accidents. If you believe they were, then you will accept the notion that Sam Giancana shot himself in the head and that John Roselli and Sam Trafficante (CIA subcontractors) "demised" themselves. President Andrew Jackson survived an assassination attempt; he claimed that the Rothschild dynastic bankers tried to kill him. His proudest achievement was to keep the Rothschilds out of our banks. At least for a time.

When the CIA kills its own, or other government agents, it uses "suicides," "natural causes," and "accidents." President Gerald Ford ordered the intelligence agencies to stop assassinating people. Following this order there were two attempts to kill President Ford — in Sacramento, and again at the St. Francis Hotel in San Francisco! Even CIA director Colby had an "accident" involving water. He had revealed to Congress "the family secrets."

The population is still dormant, frustrated, and un-organized, but when it figures out how it has been deluded, we are all in for a shock.

Lobbyists, public relations personnel, corporate lawyers, and vested interests: keep your passports handy. The airport lines will be long. There will be a day when the dynastic elite families fly their jets away. First, of course, they will transfer their electronic money abroad. It is just as well — they already bankrupted the government. The homeless and un-employed can be housed in their Long Island estates.

The national debt is war debt — our government is bankrupt. When the monetary system finally succumbs, the international bankers will introduce a silver coin called the "Amero." All they will ask in exchange will be our sovereignty. It took two world wars before the Europeans accepted the European Union and the "Euro."

My goal has been to explain what has already occurred in our society so that people might wake up and try to change the path.

My ancestors did not approve of slavery because we were once enslaved by the English. We came to the colonies as Scottish and Irish rebels attempting to escape the halter, prisons, and wars. I am a radical writer because I recognize that our mainstream media has been compromised by special interests. The banks, and media, promote social conflict and debt at the expense of you, readers.

Do not have a nice day. Read something that is factual. Entertainment is a distraction to keep us busy while our institutions decline. Talk to your neighbors — they are your friends. You have few friends left in your State Houses and Washington

Our next crisis will be a monetary crisis. Dollars will devalue and nations will purchase oil and other commodities with their own currencies or for gold.

Recently, Greece sold some of their islands to get cash to pay the interest rate on governmental debt. Most European nations, like our own, are now bankrupt. All that debt is owed to the private banking dynasties. Notice that banks control the money supply and set the interest rates on all loans and bonds. Why do they have power that should be in the hands of a national government? National policies are to be set for the good of the nation, not the bankers.

What part of "debt servitude" do citizens not understand? Student college debt is over a trillion dollars. Seventy-five per cent of college graduates now return home to live. They have limited job opportunities, yet they have debts. Congress appears gridlocked. Globalists wait for the nations to collapse and give them a kick when they can.

But Americans respond well in a crisis. The real citizens are already organizing in little groups and educating themselves. Schoolteachers can be subversive agents. They taught millions of children that we were a democracy, and some of them understand what that is supposed to mean. That dream will be a nightmare for the 1% when people decide to fight for what we were promised.

Now, what happens to your children and grandchildren will be up to you — and them. The 99% are now walking and talking. This is a worldwide phenomenon.

Reading

America's Secret Establishment, An Introduction to Skull and Bones. Antony Sutton. (The author died under suspicious circumstances. Howard Taft was the first bones man President. Bones man Bob Lovett designed Central Intelligence Agency.)

The Big White Lie, by Michael Levine.

Blood, Money, and Power. Barr McClellan.

"The Bush Crime Family," Dr. Eric Karlstrom. Article at http://www.communitycurrency.org/BushCrimeFamily.html.

Bushwhacked, by Uri Dowbenko.

Crossing the Rubicon, by Michael Ruppert, Published 2004 (Right-wing takeover)

Dark Alliance: The CIA, the Contras, and the Crack Cocaine Explosion. Gary Webb. (This stunning exposé investigates links between the cocaine trade, Nicaragua's Contra rebels, and minorities in California)

Don't Wait For The Next War. General Wesley K. Clark

The Good Old Boys: The American Elite and the Origins of the CIA. Burton Hersh. (He mentions OSS operatives that imported Nazis into intelligence agencies.) Charles Scribner's Sons. 1992.

J. Edgar Hoover, The man and his secrets. Curt Gentry. Norton Press 1991. (Blackmail, the 156 "American Liberty League" dynastic families plot to install fascism in 1933 to support their corporations.)

Killing for Land in Early California: Indian Blood at Round Valley. Frank H. Baumgardner III. Algora Publishing (2005).

The Suppressed History of American Banking: How Big Banks Fought Jackson, Killed Lincoln, and Caused the Civil War. Xaviant Haze. Bear & Company (2016)

War Against the Weak. Edwin Black. (Exposing eugenics programs; find out why you had to take an I.Q. test or achievement test in school.)

War Is a Racket by Brigadier General Smedley Darlington Butler US.M.C. (1935) Feral House.

There are plenty of books on the CIA's drug running and killing. Here are a few of them. All these books have been ignored by the privately-owned media.

Orders to Kill. William F. Pepper, (Carroll & Graff) 1995.

Powder Burns. The Squad. Michael Milan (a former hitman)

Trading With the Enemy. Charles Higham. Delacorte and Dell Press. 1983. (N.Y Times bestseller on US support for Hitler)

ENDNOTES

1   www.thenation.com/article/jfks-vietnam-withdrawal-plan-fact-not-speculation/

2   See *Orders To Kill* by William F. Pepper, Carrol & Graff Publishers, 1995

3   *The Squad,* by Michael Milan (pseudonym), Shapolsky Publishers 1989

4   www.conniescomments.blogspot.com

Printed in the United States
By Bookmasters